# Wonders of the Ocean Zoo

*By Boris Arnov, Jr. and*
*Helen Mather-Smith Mindlin*

WONDERS OF THE OCEAN ZOO

*By Helen Mather-Smith Mindlin*

DANGEROUS ISLAND

VOLCANO TRAP

# Wonders of the Ocean Zoo

by BORIS ARNOV, JR., and
HELEN MATHER-SMITH MINDLIN

ILLUSTRATED BY RUSS SMILEY

Dodd, Mead & Company • New York

American Book-Stratford Press, Inc., New York

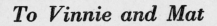

*To Vinnie and Mat*

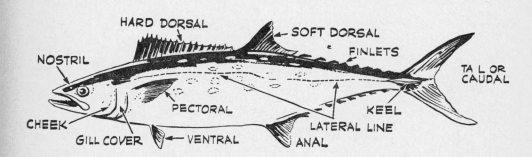

NOSTRIL

HARD DORSAL

SOFT DORSAL

FINLETS

TA L OR CAUDAL

CHEEK

GILL COVER

PECTORAL

VENTRAL

ANAL

LATERAL LINE

KEEL

DIAGRAM OF FISH

# Introduction

When you see the vast blue ocean with foamy white waves pounding on the beach, you are looking at the most unusual zoo in the world. Down in mysterious, watery depths or skimming over sandy shoals are fishes that light up like torches, some that walk and talk or are even as deadly as cobras, and monstrous creatures believed to be sea serpents.

This zoo is older than any you have seen or heard about; it was here long, long before you or I or any of our grandparents were born. Through many centuries it has been preparing its fantastic show for us.

Since its beginning, only a small part of the ocean has been explored by man. Most of it is a mystery, but in this water world certain things have been seen, just as you would see them in a zoo. Sometimes they are funny, often unusual but always interesting.

Instead of having its wild creatures penned up, as you would ordinarily see the animals at a park zoo, this ocean zoo has no bars and the inhabitants are free to swim and jump as they love to do. So perhaps if you try some alert investigating on your own, the next time you are down at the seashore, *you* might discover things that will clear up some of the strange mysteries that have puzzled man for centuries.

# Contents

*Wonders of the Ocean Zoo*

# PLANKTON

## Biggest and Tiniest

Did you know that the biggest creature in the world, the Blue Whale, eats only the tiniest food in the ocean because it has no teeth? It cannot chew and grind its food as we do but must eat the minute animals in the sea that are called Plankton.

Imagine this huge monster which can grow to be one hundred feet long and weigh over one hundred tons opening its wide mouth to suck in gallons of ocean water to get its dinner! In order to do this, it has a series of bony plates in its mouth, like hundreds of hair combs placed together, acting as a sieve, straining out and separating the billions of tiny animals that make up Plankton in the water. These bony plates are the reason why scientists call this largest animal in the world, and its other Plankton-eating relatives, the Whalebone group of whales.

The Blue Whale cruises the ocean near such widely separated places as Alaska, South Africa and California, but it is the Antarctic region that it likes the best, for here its favorite food, a tiny, shrimp-like Plankton, is most plentiful. It takes bushels and bushels of these minute animals to satisfy the hunger of one whale, yet on this diet the creature is able to grow to a mammoth size. It would be an interesting experiment for humans to eat Plankton — perhaps we might grow to weigh one hundred tons, too!

You probably wonder what the tiny Plankton eat in order to keep alive. Well, no one knows exactly; it is believed they get their nourishment from chemicals in the ocean water but, whatever their diet, they seem to thrive, for there are billions and billions of them in odd shapes and sizes. They may look like crabs, doughnuts, shrimp, hairy worms or many-pointed stars, all wriggling and swimming feebly but mostly depending on the wind and current to move them around.

The Blue Whale babies are twenty-four feet long when born and very seldom are there twins. The mother whale, being a mammal, which is any of the group of vertebrate animals that nourish their young with milk, nurses her calf for six or seven months and then teaches it to eat Plankton. After his milk diet for the first part of his life, nobody knows whether the baby Whale enjoys the change to fishy tasting Plankton, but it is known that they must agree with him, for in two years he will be very nearly as large as his parents.

Besides being handicapped by having to eat so much to nourish its huge body, the Blue Whale has other difficulties, too. For many years it has been pursued and harpooned by men in whaling ships, hunting it down for its valuable blubber, which is the fat of Whales yielding oil. This has caused the Whale to become very timid, often even being frightened by the sound of a man's voice, although it is king in size and most other creatures in the sea fear it.

It might be easier for the Whale to get along if it could eat the many kinds of fishes swimming in the ocean. But perhaps this huge mammal is lucky it has no teeth for then it would have to chase the various fishes. At least the slow-moving Plankton cannot run away.

14

## Live Sea Horns

When you arrive at Nassau, largest city in the faraway islands of the Bahamas, among the first things you see as your ship pulls into the harbor are native boys in rowboats, with Conchs piled high around them. These are soft-bodied animals that live inside of large, heavy shells. The animal itself is not very pretty, looking like a formless piece of black and pink flesh, with eyes at the ends of two long stalks. But its shell is one of the most beautiful in the ocean. It looks very much like a pinkish church, with a high, pointed, spiral steeple on one end and a broad base at the bottom, while the edge of the shell curves gracefully outward. This curving lip of the shell is especially attractive, for it is colored a vivid pink and glistens like a pearl. The inside part of the shell is smooth and satiny, and the live animal, which is all muscle, stays cozily curled up there, with its body firmly attached and twisted to fit to the upper part of the church steeple.

15

The native boys of Nassau dive many times into the ocean to gather all these Conchs until their small boats are so filled with them that it seems as if they would capsize. You may have guessed that these boys sell the Conchs, and if you were in Nassau where ships come in most every day, you would probably be doing the very same thing. It is a quick way to make spending money while at the same time having the fun of diving. There is always a ready market with tourists, who want the lovely pink shells as curios, and with the natives, who eat the animals themselves.

Conchs are found in other places, too, such as along the warm coast of Florida. Down on the floor of the ocean, they live their quiet, uneventful lives. They never leave their shells which increase in size as the animals inside grow larger and they move around by reaching out a long muscle called a foot, pushing themselves along with a series of leaps as they turn the shell from side to side. They eat dead animal matter, gathering it on the bottom of the ocean, and they seem to be peace-loving creatures, never fighting among themselves or with other dwellers of the deep.

In the tropics, everybody likes to eat Conchs — the natives who cook them into delicious soup or fry them to a golden brown and the fishes that try to catch a careless one sticking out too far from its shell. As long as a Conch stays inside its house, it is protected against everything except man, who must use a hammer to break through the heavy shell.

In the olden days, the Conch shell was used as a horn, because the sound made by blowing into it can be heard for a great distance. Shepherds would call their sheep together and Indians would use it to signal from one far place to another. So if you ever have a Conch shell, be sure to try blowing into it. You'll be very surprised at the deep, wailing sound that comes from it.

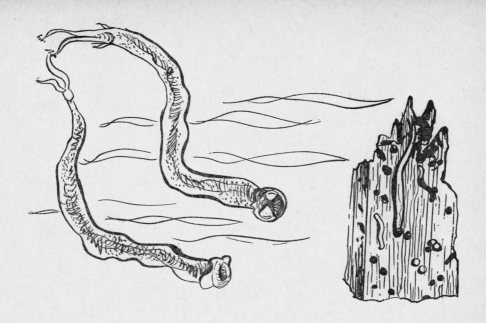

## Enemy of All Ships

Have you ever heard about the Shipworm, one of the most destructive creatures in the ocean? This harmless looking animal has caused more damage over the years than all other sea catastrophes, such as ships sunk in storms, docks wrecked by bombs of war, and vessels lost in collisions. Enough of them together can bore through the bottom of a boat and sink it in three months, or honeycomb the heavy pilings of a dock, causing it to tumble down. Shipworms probably have no idea that they are responsible for all this destruction. They are just hungry and homeless and they get both food and shelter by boring head first into submerged wood.

Teredos — the fancy name for Shipworms — are very well equipped to carry on their strange lives. At the front of their long, soft, unprotected bodies are two small curved shell plates that lie alongside the head. This shell surface is lined with rows of fine teeth, looking very much like a miniature saw. This is just the thing for cutting away at the wood as the animal digs.

If Shipworms would only make a racket as they chomp and chew, you would at least know that they are in the bottom of your boat, but they work silently and it is only when a vessel is hauled out of the water that you can see how much of it has been eaten away. And if you look closely at the wood, you will find two tunnels for each Teredo. These tunnels are lined with a hard, shell-like substance that the Shipworm secretes from its body. One tunnel draws in water for breathing and the other is used to expel it, along with the waste products.

A Shipworm may lay as many as one hundred million eggs, and when they hatch, the babies swim around until they find a place suitable for burrowing the rest of their lives. Can't you just see the house hunting going on below the water as each little Shipworm tries to get the best spot of wood?

In ancient days, Shipworms were a great bother, too, and the Greeks coated their ships' bottoms with lead sheathing, while others used pitch and tar. Now, in modern times, we use creosote and copper paints on submerged wood, and although it does not stop the damage entirely, it does help. A hungry Shipworm might approach a new dock piling saying, "Aha! A nice breakfast. I'll see if I like the flavor." But if the wood has been freshly treated with copper paint, the worm probably says, "*Ugh!* This is not for me. I'll try some other wood." And it goes on its way.

But everyone does not try to get rid of Shipworms. In Thailand, they are considered especially good to eat and the natives put soft pieces of wood in the water and wait until the worms bore in. Then, gathering the wood, they feast upon the worms. In Australia, Shipworms can grow to six feet in length. You can picture how overjoyed any aborigine would be who might find one this size, for it would make quite a meal for his family!

## Live Building Blocks

The rock-like Corals, found in both cold and warm seas, are not rocks at all but the skeletons of many dead and live animals. They are different from most other animals because, instead of having their skeletons *inside* of their bodies, they have them on the *outside*.

Great numbers of these Corals pile up on top of one another, each making a hard limestone skeleton around itself. This skeleton is both its home and prison and every Coral joins its neighbor which is doing exactly the same thing. As the animal grows, the skeleton around it grows, too, until millions of live ones are stacked on top of their ancestors, reaching so high that they form in warm seas what is known as a Coral Reef. In time, if seaweed and earth gather on this reef, trees and plants may begin to grow, so that eventually it all might form an island. Because Corals use their own bodies to construct their homes, they are really live building blocks.

19

Coral animals grow into many unusual shapes, such as Tree Coral, which has branches and a trunk; Brain Coral, which is round with creases running through it; Staghorn Coral, which looks like horns; and others that have the appearance of fine lace. There are even some shaped like cabbages and cauliflower and the underside of mushrooms. Many are colored in lovely shades, such as purple, pink, yellow or rose, and you would think that some Coral beds were flower or vegetable gardens. After Coral is bleached in the sun, it becomes a snowy white and very often it is dyed to give it the same color it once had in the ocean.

In order to eat, Corals move their tentacles about, reaching for microscopic sea life. These tentacles, lined with many stinging cells, first paralyze these minute animals, after which the Corals carry them to their mouths. During the day, Corals shrink inside their limestone houses. They stick their tentacles out only at night, in order to feed, for if Corals are exposed to sunlight or air they will die.

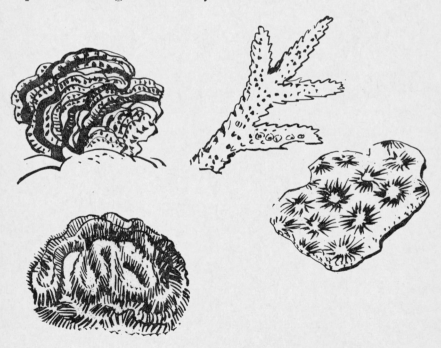

# Ocean Eggs

A chicken gets awfully excited about laying only one egg, loudly announcing it to the whole world, while in the ocean a fish may silently lay thousands of eggs at a time, usually without anyone knowing when or where this spawning takes place. The cackling hen has most everyone believing its eggs are the best tasting, but there are a great many people in the world who think that eggs from the ocean are the most delicious of all.

Natives in the South Seas even claim that a certain worm's eggs are better than any other. These come from the Palolo Worm, a mysterious underwater creature that lives its whole life at the bottom of the ocean. Here it stays, head first in a hole of the coral reef, never venturing into open water or near the surface.

The Palolo Worm grows to three inches in length and it is very thin, looking much like the common earthworm. It has feelers on its head and a few bristles on its body. Its life is quiet and uneventful until, one morning of each year, an amazing thing takes place when the time comes for it to lay its eggs.

The natives know that the Palolo Worm will spawn at dawn, one week after the full moon in November, every year. This is a time for great rejoicing, as preparations are made for a special feast. The natives set out in their canoes, carrying large woven leaf baskets to hold all the eggs they collect from the deep-sea barnyard.

The Palolo Worm's eggs have been developing from the back part of its body and they resemble a string of beads which can be several times longer than the worm itself. Finally, the time arrives when the eggs are ripe and these break loose from the worm's body and come floating to the surface of the water. The ripe eggs look like pieces of spaghetti and in the pale light of dawn they are quickly gathered by the waiting natives. It is quite an honor for the first canoe that gets back to shore with its load of eggs. These are eaten raw or roasted . . . but some always escape to hatch into more Palolo Worms.

These are not the only ocean eggs that people eat. In England, Alaska and Italy Sea Urchins are gathered. This animal, which is about the size of a tennis ball with a thin shell surrounding it, is found in the water near rocky places. The ripe eggs removed from these Urchins are considered a great delicacy.

Then, of course, there are delicious eggs from many kinds of fishes, and they are called roe. Shad are caught as they leave the ocean to go up the rivers to spawn, and their roe, which is especially good eating, is on sale in many markets. The eggs from Salmon are canned and sold at high prices with the fancy name of caviar. Even the fishes themselves like to eat the Salmon eggs which are used as bait by many anglers.

If you should happen to catch a fish during its spawning time, be sure to look inside for the roe. It will be laid out neatly in the region below the fish's backbone. If you eat the roe and see how good it tastes, then you, too, may become an egg hunter of the sea.

## Reef Fishes

Some fishes that roam the ocean are like traveling gypsies, always on the move and sleeping each night in a different place. Others are stay-at-homes that prefer reefs with their many holes and caves, which make wonderful hiding places. You will usually find the same fishes around the same reefs for a very long time, unless, of course, they are gobbled up by bigger fish. Warm waters of oceans are where the Reef Fishes are found and they are usually very colorful.

The Beau Gregory, one of these tropical reef dwellers, is a nervous little fish that grows to be about two inches long. It is beautifully colored, its front part a bright blue and the back and belly a vivid yellow, with a dark spot on the dorsal fin.

In spite of being such a tiny fish, the Beau Gregory is a born fighter. It lives alone in a hole in the reef, chasing away any other fishes that come near. Strangely enough, it will not even allow another Beau Gregory to share its home, except during breeding season. At the least sign of danger, it darts into its hole. This usually has not only an entrance, but an exit, too, which is used if the fish wants to make a fast getaway.

A Beau Gregory makes an excellent pet in a salt-water home aquarium, and if you happen to be in Florida, you can catch one yourself. All you need is a fine-meshed net attached to a long handle, and plenty of patience, for at low tide these spunky fish are often found only a few feet from shore.

In order for your Beau Gregory to remain alive, it must be kept in a fish bowl with clean ocean water, and you should feed it a pinch of prepared fish food every day. This little pet will overcome its natural nervousness and desire to fight and learn to eat out of your hand. It will even come to the surface of its bowl, looking as if it is trying to attract attention by blowing bubbles. It will play with its own reflection on the side of the fish bowl hour after hour. But you must have a clean shell or piece of coral in the bottom of the tank, for the Beau Gregory may become frightened and want to dart into it for cover, just as it does in the ocean.

Sergeant Majors are another kind of Reef Fish that grow to three or four inches in length. They are exactly opposite the Beau Gregories by nature, because they love company and are always found in a group with forty or fifty others of their own kind. They swim above the reef and use its holes and crevices only when something really frightens them. None of these hiding places are very satisfactory, for they do not have them planned in advance, as have the Beau Gregories.

The attractive up-and-down stripes of the Sergeant Majors are black on their yellow bodies, which give them a military appearance. This is why they are named for an army officer. These fish also make excellent pets in a salt water home aquarium and they are a lot of fun to keep.

Probably the hungriest of the Reef Fishes are the Snappers. They are a beautiful gray to reddish color on their sides, with black stripes running through their eyes. They can grow to weigh several pounds and

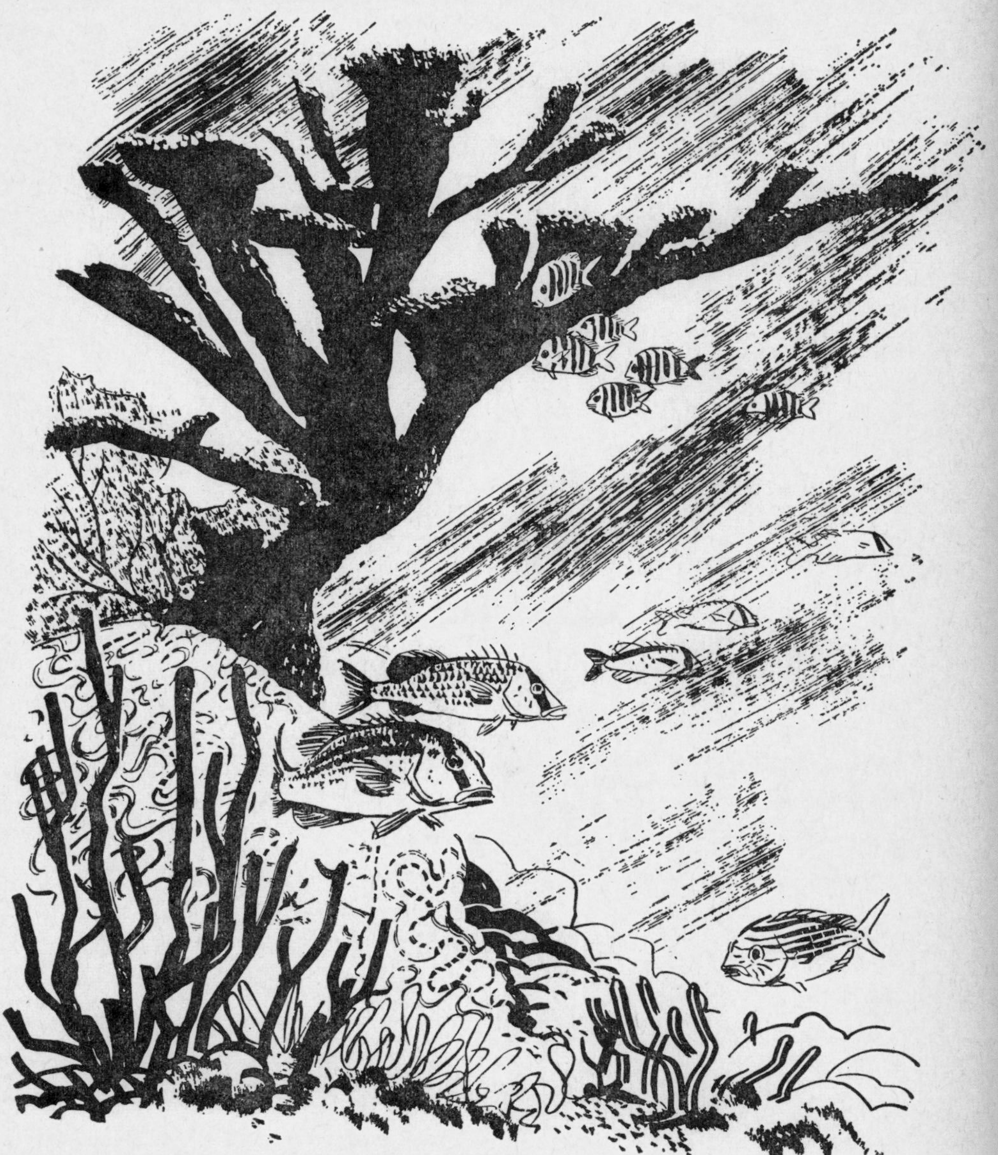

have sharp teeth coming out of their jaws. Often they move in large schools, and other times there are just a few together. They never stay in one particular spot as the Beau Gregories do, but move around the reef like bandits, always ready to grab anything that looks good enough to eat. Their sharp teeth and the way they quickly snap their jaws on everything has given them the name of Snappers.

There are many more Reef Fishes besides the ones we have told you about, and they all eat small living things in the water, or even dead matter that they scavenge. They are not fussy and will eat most anything they can get. All are egg layers, and although not exactly friendly to each other, they at least live their separate lives in and around the reef without too much fighting.

The coloring of most Reef Fishes is strikingly beautiful and it seems as if an artist had spent long hours with a paint brush, decorating each one. Even your mother's prettiest dress cannot compare with the colors and designs found in Reef Fishes, for man-made art is never as beautiful as Nature's.

All Reef Fishes have one thing in common — they are very curious. If something unusual or new comes near the reef, they will peek from their hiding places just the same as you would look out of your window if you saw a funny-looking stranger walk down the street where you live.

## The Lazy Hitch-Hiking Fish

If you have ever seen a piece of an automobile tire with its criss-cross markings, you know what the top of a Remora's head looks like, for this strange fish uses the large, flat surface on its head as a suction disc and will attach itself to a Swordfish, Shark or any other large fish that might be around.

In this way, the Remora not only catches a free ride but also has its meals served, for when the larger fish is busy eating, this hitch-hiking fish quickly lets loose and rushes out to grab the pieces and bits floating in the water. The big fish does not seem to mind that the Remora is hitch-hiking, for it never makes an attempt to eat it.

Sometimes a Remora will cling to the smooth side of a small boat. There is an ancient legend that an emperor's death was caused by his great galley being slowed down by a Remora which had attached itself to the hull. This allowed the enemy to catch up with the emperor while the remainder of his fleet escaped.

If you take a Remora out of water, it will cling to your wet hand with its suction disc, and its hold is so powerful that you will have to slide it sideways to loosen it. In Australia and some Oriental countries, fishermen have put this to good use. A light line is placed around the Remora's tail and it then becomes a sort of fishhook. It is tossed into the ocean and left there until it finds a larger fish or turtle to attach itself to. Then both the Remora and the animal it is clinging to are pulled in.

Often the life of a Remora is very exciting, as when the big fish to which it is attached races around the ocean, taking it on a fast, zigzag roller-coaster ride. Other fishes may be envious of the Remora and the way it has solved transportation and eating problems, but there is a bad side to this kind of lazy life. There are times when the Remora's transportation gets into a fight and the hitch-hiking fish is most uncomfortable. Or often the big fish is killed and the Remora must find a new home. So you can see that the life of this lazy fish is not always a joy ride!

## Original Jet

Down in the deep, dark water of warm oceans lives the Octopus, one of the homeliest creatures in existence. It has a large, repulsive head, a fierce-looking mouth, with a pair of powerful horny jaws shaped much like a parrot's beak. Its eyes are set close together on top of its ugly beak, and some say they shine with a vicious expression when the creature is angry, scaring the daylights out of anyone around. Besides having such an odd head, its body is even stranger, with eight long arms that look like wriggling snakes, each one with many suckers.

Because of its appearance, the Octopus is claimed to be the most evil and dangerous animal in the sea. It is even said that because it has a bad temper and is so hard to get along with, it lives alone, just like a hermit, in an underwater cave in the rocks.

But all the unpleasant things that are believed about the Octopus are not true, for it is really a coward. It will usually run from you in fear, or, if there happens to be a shell around, it will try to hide inside. It will not give battle to man unless angered or injured and only then, if it is forced to, will it fight to the finish, trying to pull its enemy down beneath the water.

Although the Octopus can move rapidly over sand and rocks with the use of its suckers and eight arms, the most amazing thing about it is the way it swims. Sucking in water through its long syphon tube and expelling it with great force, it moves swiftly backwards. It goes through the water in almost the same way that a jet plane flies through the air — which makes the Octopus the originator of jet propulsion!

When the Octopus hunts for its food, it hides under some rocks until a fish or crab passes by and then it darts out, grabbing up its dinner and killing it with its strong, beak jaws. But when the Octopus itself is hunted as food, that is a different story, for it uses all kinds of clever methods to keep from being caught. It can change color before your very eyes, so that it looks like the surrounding rocks as it squeezes way back into a deep cave. If these tricks fail, it has one other way to outwit its enemy. You can do it yourself without being an Octopus. Just take a few drops of writing ink and spill them into a glass of water. You will see how cloudy the clear water immediately becomes. Well, the Octopus does this very same thing, discharging a dark colored fluid which acts as a smoke screen so that it is able to make a fast escape.

## Fishes That Talk

You may think that the only sounds in the ocean are those of the pounding waves, but wouldn't you get the surprise of your life if you could listen in on all the other noises in the sea, for there are squealing, grunting, croaking and humming sounds in the water, just as there are dogs barking and birds chirping on land. Most of these sea sounds must be listened to with a special kind of underwater microphone, and then you would hear so much racket that it would sound like a busy downtown street.

Soon you would learn that the Croaker is the noisiest fish of all, making a sound like the rapid beating of a drum. The Horse Mackerel, the

Sun Fish and certain Trigger Fishes make sounds like teeth grating together. The Grunts make loud noises that resemble a bull frog with a bad cold trying to croak. And, as you might guess, the Hog Fish grunts just like a pig. One of the funniest noises comes from the Sea Robin, for it has a strange cackle that makes you think it belongs in a barnyard instead of in the deep ocean. There is even one, the Toadfish, that lets out something like the blast of a boat whistle. And when shrimp are in large groups, they make a humming noise which seems very much like the swarming of bees. If all these fishy noises were put together in an orchestra, there would be an awful jumble of sound but not much music.

The sea animals make these noises in order to frighten away an enemy or when they themselves feel fear. They also talk to one another, and if you could understand their language, you might hear a Croaker, as it rolls out its drum-beat, say, "Did you know that a fishing boat sank right near here? Let's all go over and see if there are any choice pieces of food floating around."

Or a Horse Mackerel might grumble, "Can't we have any peace and quiet in the ocean? Why are those noisy Croakers always drumming and why do the Toadfish keep blasting out with their whistles? A law should be passed against all this bedlam!"

In order to produce all these peculiar sounds, some fishes force air through tiny tubes which lead into an air sac. Others vibrate their gill covers against the sides of their heads. Some even use a special row of teeth, set way back in their throats, which they grind together.

When the men of the United States Navy tried out the underwater microphone and first heard the terrific racket in the ocean, they must have thought for sure that they had discovered an enemy submarine! But they soon found out there was no danger. It was just sea animals carrying on their everyday life. In order not to make this same mistake again, the Navy scientists recorded all these different sounds on records, and so found that fishes talk, in their own way, the same as humans.

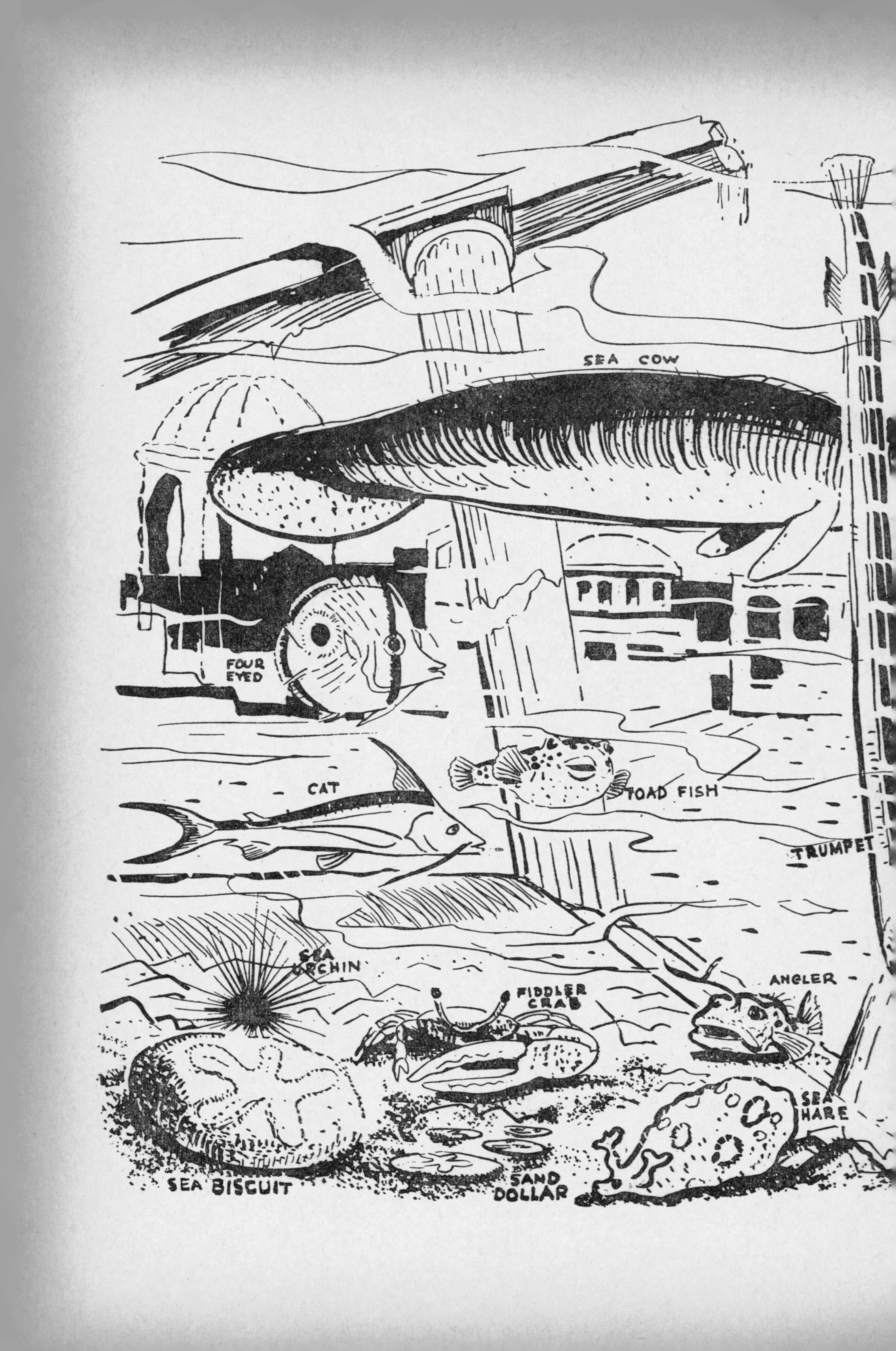
SEA COW
FOUR EYED
CAT
TOAD FISH
TRUMPET
SEA URCHIN
FIDDLER CRAB
ANGLER
SEA HARE
SEA BISCUIT
SAND DOLLAR

## Fish City

For hundreds of years it has been supposed that underneath the ocean, somewhere near Europe, a lost continent lies. It is referred to as Atlantis, and some people think it was once a city that sank during a great disaster.

Imagine coming upon a whole city under the water, with buildings and streets, parks and playgrounds but with no people! Perhaps the creatures who live in the ocean know about this city and even use it, just as the artist has pictured it on these pages.

## Ocean Bandit

As you grow older and larger, you will outgrow all your clothes — but your house will always be big enough for you — even if you come to be seven feet tall and weigh three hundred pounds. You will never have to worry about finding another house every time you expand an inch. But all growing creatures are not as lucky as you, and one of these is a little ocean dweller called a Hermit Crab.

This animal is really a bandit, for it spends its whole life stealing shells. Born without any shelter of its own to protect its soft body and long claws, this odd crab soon found out that it would be a lot safer with a hard shell over it in time of danger.

The big problem, of course, was not only in finding the first shell for protection but also in discovering a way to keep on getting a new home as it outgrew the old one. That is why, in order to keep up with its growing needs, the Hermit Crab became a highwayman!

First, it finds one of its own kind already curled up inside a stolen shell, perhaps a snail shell. Then it pokes a claw into the shell, almost as if it had a gun and was holding up the other Hermit Crab. This often leads to a fight. If the bandit is unsuccessful in making the other crab vacate its shell, it will go on to find an empty one. This time, it gropes around inside the shell, exploring it carefully to determine whether it is roomy enough to take the place of the one on its back, already outgrown. Once satisfied, quick as a flash, it leaves its own old home to dart into the new one. This same sort of transfer goes on over and over again.

The female Hermit Crab protects her eggs by carrying them stuck to her own body. But after they are hatched, the babies drift away and take care of themselves. Just a few live, out of the many born, and these are faced with the same problem as their parents — to find a comfortable, hard shell to protect their tender bodies.

Whether you are on the Atlantic or the Pacific Ocean, you will probably find these queer-looking crabs, scurrying around on the floor of the sea, eating little bits of living or dead animal matter. They always carry their shell houses on their backs and are continually curious about everything, sticking their heads out to see what is going on. You might even see one perform a trick which is very cute and clever. If the Hermit Crab is in danger and happens to be on a rock, it withdraws quickly into its shell and starts tumbling and rolling, faster and faster, until it is out of reach of its enemy.

# White Fox

Most every animal in the ocean has a way to protect itself. Some use camouflage, others are vicious fighters and a few, like the Bonefish, depend entirely on speed to get away from danger. When these stream-lined fish swim through the water they seem as fast as a streak of lightning. Even the water is in their way when they are in a hurry, so, instead of slicing *through* it as most fishes do, they *push* it ahead of them. You can see a wave of water moving in front of a Bonefish if it is swimming rapidly.

The Bonefish is shaped almost like a bullet and it is an off-white color, with faint stripes along its sides. It is as scary and clever as a fox and from this animal it gets its Latin name — *Albula vulpes*, which means white fox. The species is found mostly in the warm waters of the Hawaiian Islands, the West Indies and Florida. In Hawaii, fishermen get them weighing up to twenty-five pounds.

If you want to catch a Bonefish, which is one of the most exciting sports in the world, be prepared for a difficult job. It has been figured that every Bonefish caught costs on the average of five hundred dollars, considering all the people who buy equipment and hire guides and boats for the pursuit.

First, you find places in shallow water where crabs and shrimp hide in the sand and weeds. Then, moving very quietly, you watch for a Bonefish to "tail." This means it is standing on its nose as it roots about on the bottom, hunting for food, with its tail sticking up out of the water. Trying not to make a noise and hardly breathing, you throw your shrimp bait over near it, hoping it won't scare away. The Bonefish sees a nice, fat shrimp on the hook, cautiously picks it up, is hooked, and immediately streaks off like a rocket.

If the White Fox had stuck to the hard work of getting its dinner, searching the sand and grass, instead of picking up your easily gotten bait, it would not have been caught. But I guess the Bonefish is like many people who don't like to work too hard!

## Dancing Fish

If you saw a group of fish swim out of the ocean, come up on shore and dance around on their tails, you would probably think something was wrong and try to throw them back into the water. Well, don't be concerned, for these are Grunion and they know just what they are doing.

It sounds almost too fantastic — a seven-inch fish that dances on its tail out of water — but it is true! Another peculiar thing about these Grunion is that they are found nowhere else in the world except on the shore of California. Perhaps they prefer the climate there, just as some people flock to certain ocean resorts.

To see these small, silvery Grunion actually lay their eggs, you must first know that they come up on the beaches only on certain nights of high tide, from March through August. At fifteen minutes before the crest of the high tide, there will be thousands of them in the ocean and with each breaking wave they swim up the gently sloping beach. When they have arrived high enough up on the shore, the females bury their tails in the sand in order to lay their eggs — which actually makes the fish stand upright. You would think this ought to take a long time, but within twenty or thirty seconds the Grunion come up with one wave, spawn and then return to the sea with the wash of the next breaker. All this happens so fast that strangers watching hardly realize what is taking place.

There are many who do know about the habits of Grunion at spawning time, however, and they crowd the beaches during the nights the fish come up on shore. They have lots of fun catching them — if they are quick enough — but the real treat comes later, when the fish are fried to a crisp brown.

For the next two weeks, the tide remains low along that beach and well away from the fish nursery, and the sand-covered eggs are kept warm by the sun. Then high tide comes again and, as the water pounds and churns, the buried eggs are dug out by the waves. They hatch immediately, and, like their parents, the baby fish swim into the sea, coming back to shore only when they are full-grown and ready to lay eggs themselves.

Grunion are one of the unknown mysteries of the ocean. Why are they found only on California shores? How does the female Grunion know just where to lay the eggs so that the high tide that comes two weeks later will release the hidden eggs from the sand and help them to be born? Perhaps when you grow up you might become an ichthyologist — which means a person who studies fishes — and find the answers to the life story of Grunion and many other strange fishes, too.

## Sea Elephants

Imagine coming face to face in the ocean with a huge animal that weighs two tons, is fifteen feet long and has an extremely long nose! You would probably think you were dreaming, but this creature really does exist. The large nose, which is found only on the males, hangs limply most of the time, falling into its mouth when it yawns or barks. However, when the animal becomes excited, its funny nose stretches to an enormous size. That is why it is called the Sea Elephant.

These gigantic animals are the largest of the seal family and most of them live around the island of Guadalupe, which is off the coast of Lower California and near Mexico. There are other relatives, even larger — often growing to eighteen feet around the waist — that live in the Antarctic.

Like a great many other air-breathing mammals of the ocean, Sea Elephants are born with a problem. They cannot stay under water for longer than seven minutes. Then they must come up to gulp fresh air, so they divide their lives between land and water. At night, they feed in the ocean, diving as deep down as three hundred feet, where they eat their favorite foods of squid, rat fish, skate, puffer shark and sometimes seaweed. During the day, the Sea Elephants stay on the warm, sandy shores, stretched out in the sun, barking to one another as they carry on a conversation, back and forth. If the sun gets too hot, they sprinkle sand on their backs by throwing it up with their hind flippers, or they retreat into the coolness of caves.

For centuries, Sea Elephants led a lazy and uneventful life, dwelling in great colonies, eating, sleeping and raising their young. Then one day it was found that their blubber or fat was almost pure oil and even more valuable for lubricating machinery than the oil of the Sperm Whale. Immediately, the Sea Elephants were slaughtered by the thousands, which was an easy task, for they did not know what it meant to be afraid of man. They became so scarce that the United States and Mexico passed laws which made it a crime to kill a Sea Elephant.

Even now, on the island of Guadalupe, a garrison of Mexican soldiers is stationed permanently. Their duty is to keep everyone off that island and protect the small number of animals that are left. This is a lucky thing for the Sea Elephants, as they are unable to protect themselves. All they can do in self-defense is puff up their long noses and throw sand in your eyes with their hind flippers. Of course, if one should fall on you with its two tons of solid blubber, it wouldn't be very comfortable, but a Sea Elephant does not seem to know how dangerous its own weight might prove — or maybe it is just a peace-loving animal and does not want to hurt anyone.

# Masquerading Spider

There are many kinds of crabs in the ocean but one in particular, the Horseshoe Crab, is probably the funniest looking of all. It has a reddish-black shell, with the head part shaped like a horse's hoof and the body tapering to a spine tail which is sometimes as long as two feet. The underpart of this strange animal looks like a spider, which it should, for it is not a crab at all but really belongs to the spider family.

The Horseshoe Crab is found mostly in the shallow waters and along the muddy beaches of the Atlantic and Pacific Oceans. Here it digs in the sand, using its head as a shovel, trying to find the soft marine worms it eats. If somehow this crab is turned over on its back, it simply sticks its dagger-like tail in the sand and flips its body right side up again.

It is very easy to catch a Horseshoe Crab — if you watch out for the wicked-looking spine tail — and in Malaya, China, Japan and the Philippines they are eaten as food. In the East Indies, the natives make use of every part of this crab, just as we do with every part of the pig. They eat the flesh and use the spine tail as tips for lances and arrows, while the hollow empty shell serves as a water pan. In this country, where we do not need the parts of the Horseshoe Crab for any of these things, they are used only as a fertilizer.

# Little Serpents

For hundreds of years there was a mystery of the sea that no one could understand and it is only recently — in our generation — that some parts of this great mystery have been solved. It is the remarkable story of fresh water Eels.

These Eels are a dark grayish color and look like snakes, and although they are really fish, they swim through the water with wave-like motions just as snakes move on the ground. They are not dangerous like their cousins, the Moray Eels, that live in ocean reefs.

The strangest thing about these river Eels is that each autumn they take part in an amazing mass migration. At spawning time, they journey from rivers and streams into the Atlantic Ocean.

Suddenly, as if someone had given a signal, all the fresh water Eels in Europe and North America leave their homes, which are often many miles up rivers, and swim downstream toward the salty sea. They leave by the thousands as they head directly for the ocean. Then the strange mystery begins! Once the Eels are in the open waters of the Atlantic, they completely disappear.

Men puzzled over this way back in ancient times: Where do the fresh water Eels go to spawn after they have left the rivers? Why, in the spring, do just baby Eels come back up the rivers, but never the adult ones?

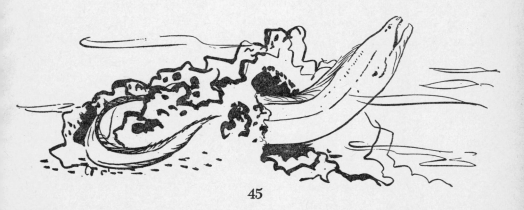

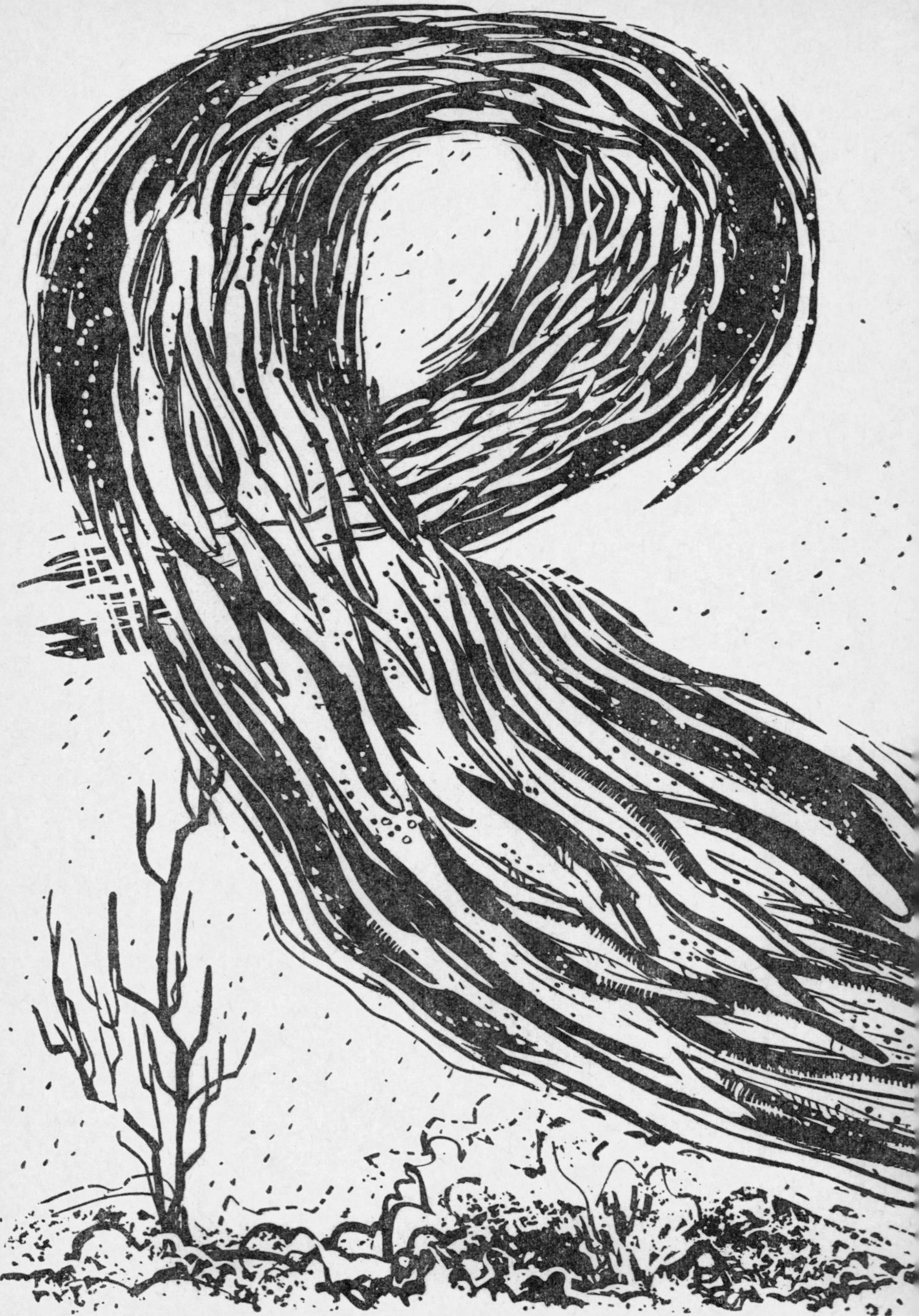

There are a great many Eels eaten as food — which, naturally, provides a living for the hundreds of fishermen who catch them — so the governments of different countries decided to study them. They set up regular detective bureaus on the high seas to try to find out about the spawning habits of Eels. Captains of commercial ships on the Atlantic were given fine-meshed nets and asked to catch new-born Eels, if they could find them. Above all, they were to try and help discover where Eels are born. Besides the commercial ships, there were hundreds of research vessels with scientists aboard who were also tracking down the habits of Eels. All this took place over a period of many years.

If you will look at a map of the Atlantic Ocean, you will find an area called the Sargasso Sea. At last it was discovered that here, around this region, was the spawning place of Eels.

At these breeding grounds, southeast of Bermuda, the sea becomes filled with wriggling Eels that have just finished their long autumn journey from the streams and rivers of Europe by some unknown route. And in the breeding grounds to the south of Bermuda are found the Eels from North America, having also arrived at their destination by an unknown route. The Eels of both continents keep apart from one another, but all answer that mysterious call that takes them from their fresh water homes through thousands of miles of ocean to their own particular meeting spot near the Sargasso Sea.

After a while the adult Eels disappear, never to be seen again. Perhaps they die or maybe they live out the rest of their lives near the bottom of the ocean. But no adult Eel has ever been seen returning to its original fresh water home.

Sometime later, tiny, leaf-shaped, transparent animals appear at the spawning grounds. It took many more years for scientists to discover that these were the baby Eels. And they also found that there was a slight difference between the North American and the European Eels. These babies depend upon the currents to push them along. The European baby Eels drift toward the coast of Europe, the home of their parents. The North American baby Eels drift toward North America, the continent from which their parents came. All eat Plankton, the microscopic animals in the sea. By their second year, the European babies turn into long, thin shaped Eels called Elvers. The North American Eels become Elvers by their first year. At last they look like miniatures of their parents and are ready and able to swim up the rivers.

In the spring, the Elvers move into the fresh waters of rivers and streams. Then, again, Eels surprise you by doing something very unusual. The males and females separate and do not mix again until the time comes for the mass migration into the sea. The males stay in the brackish waters near the river mouths and the females swim far upstream into headwaters. Both males and females are tremendously hungry and they eat crabs, shrimps, worms, fishes, snails and water plants. And although the females have a longer distance to travel, they grow to four feet, but the males reach only half this length.

There are Eels in the Pacific Ocean, too, but nothing is known about their life history. It may take many more years, but in time we hope to find out everything there is to know about the interesting life of Eels.

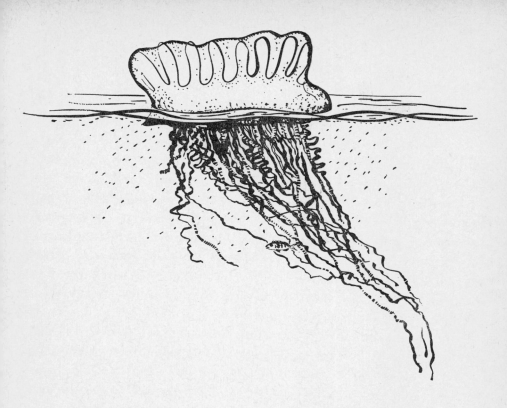

## The Beautiful, Dangerous Man-o'-War

It is hard to believe that anything as beautiful as the Man-o'-War can be so unpleasant if you happen to touch it. This special kind of jellyfish has a bright blue float which keeps it on the water's surface and, with its long, streamer-like tentacles dangling below, it looks like some kind of exotic, tropical flower. You would never suspect that its waving tentacles are covered with poison stinging cells.

You might wonder why this jellyfish has the name Man-o'-War, but if you have ever seen pictures of old-time battleships with the same name sailing before a breeze, you will know that the Man-o'-War's float is very much like one of these sails. The float continuously changes shape as it trims itself to catch the wind, helping the animal to sail across many miles of ocean. The tentacles, which may be forty or fifty feet long, not only act as an anchor to keep the float from being blown too swiftly, but they are also used to catch food.

In the open sea, a little fish may see the Man-o'-War's tentacles and try to hide in them for protection from larger fish. This is a mistake, for the spear-pointed stinging cells on the pretty tentacles immediately paralyze it and it is slowly pulled toward the Man-o'-War's sucking mouth. The unfortunate little fish was deceived into believing it would be safe when really it swam right into a death trap.

Sometimes a bather will swim into a Man-o'-War without seeing it and he feels as if a swarm of bees had stung him. Although not deadly, the poison in the stinging cells can make him most uncomfortable for a long while.

The strangest part of a Man-o'-War's life has to do with a little purplish fish that lives among the poison tentacles, darting in and out, eating the scraps of food left by its host. This tiny fish is never injured by the Man-o'-War and no one has solved the mystery of their unusual relationship. Has it learned to dodge the tentacles with their stinging cells, or is it simply that the poison does not hurt it? As a matter of fact, it even acts as a lure to coax other fish into the Man-o'-War's trap.

I'm sure you will agree that this is one of the most peculiar partnerships you ever heard of.

# Trap-Door Snails

Periwinkles are creatures of the sea that must stay out of the sea. They would die if they tried to live in the ocean, but are unable to stay alive entirely away from it. The Periwinkles solve this problem by attaching themselves to rocks on the shore which actually keep them out of the water but allow them to be close enough to get the sea spray. In this way they keep their gills wet and are able to live their whole lives without ever drying out.

Periwinkles grow to the size of a small lima bean and they live in spiral-shaped shell houses on the rocky shores of warm oceans. They are so well camouflaged to look like the rocks that it is hard to see them.

A Periwinkle never leaves its house, which has a trap door fixed so that when the animal pulls inside its shell, this door shuts so tightly that no air or ocean water can come inside. When a Periwinkle wants to eat, it uses its little file-like tongue to scrape the rocks for the microscopic plants it feeds upon.

The Periwinkle nurseries are located in rock weeds where the babies hold on to the plants. And isn't this a grand place for a nursery, for when the weeds wave and bend with the currents, the baby Periwinkles probably have a perfect rocking cradle!

## Fishes That Walk

You will have to run very fast if you want to see fishes that walk, and if you do catch up with them, you will witness one of the most unusual sights in the world. Little five-inch fish called Blennies leave their homes in the shallow pools of the outgoing tide to come out on dry land, where they hop and skip over the rocks. Here they hunt for their favorite food, a green plant covering the rocks, called algae. You may see thousands of them grazing as cattle do in a pasture, and you will be very much surprised to learn that they do all their walking without any feet.

Instead of legs and feet, these cute little Blennies stand up on their pectoral fins, which are located near their undersides. With the help of their tails, they can move about on land with amazing speed. Besides being able to outrun you in a race over the rocks, these tiny fish have remarkable eyes which stick out above the level of their heads so that they can see you coming seventy-five feet away and scamper off before you can grab them.

There are other fishes, too, that walk on land almost as fast as they swim in the ocean. These are Gobies, Serpent Heads and certain Cat Fish. And there is one, the Sea Robin, that swims like other fish, walks along the sea bottom, talks by making a cackling sound, and can even spread its large pectoral fins to go flying through the air. It certainly would be fun to have one of these for a pet!

Then there are skipping Gobies that live among the mangrove roots on wet mucky beaches of tropical seas. These can remain alive out of water for an entire day. They have thick skins which hold in their body moisture, protecting them against the sun. They skip around on land, looking very much like tiny lizards, as they hunt for their favorite food of insects. In case of danger, they quickly dive into burrows, which they have already dug by biting into the mud and carrying it to the surface in their mouths.

Even though it sounds almost unbelievable, these fish that walk on land have special breathing organs and the linings of their mouths are modified for breathing air.

Wouldn't it be interesting to put these walking fish in a sideshow, for they are just as odd as the fat lady or the fire-eating man of a circus.

## *Angelfish and Devilfish*

There is no stranger looking creature in the sea than the Manta Ray or, as it is often called, the Devilfish. It has long curling fins growing from its flat head and these look like the horns of a wild bull. Its body is shaped as if it had great, bat-like wings and, with its long, thin, whip-like tail, it is unlike any fish you could ever imagine.

The Manta's horns are really fins, although they look like leathery muscle tissue. When it dashes into a school of fish, these fins are of great assistance in helping it get its dinner. It waves them about as a boxer does, in a constant whirling motion, using them to sweep prey into its mouth.

A Manta Ray can leap five feet out of the water and, as it often grows as big as a full-sized elephant, its sudden jump from the sea is an awe-inspiring sight. The noise made by its body as it falls back into the water sounds like the shot of a cannon and can be heard several miles away. It would not be very wise to get in the way of one when it is jumping, would it?

There are reports of Manta Rays becoming entangled in anchor chains, but this seems to present no problem for them at all, because they have tremendous strength. They simply wrap their horns around the chain, lift up the heavy anchor as if it were a feather and start swimming away with the anchor, pulling the ship behind them. Considering the terror that this causes among the crew, and the fact that this huge monster has such long curling horns, it is not surprising that it has been given the name of Devilfish. But Manta Rays are really not mean animals at all, and they will never bother you if you leave them alone.

Opposite in looks to the Manta Ray, and growing as large as a dinner plate, is the Queen Angelfish. It has a sweet, angelic expression on its face and a highly colored body, with a blend of bright blue and vivid yellow and a blue ring on the top of its head like a crown. Instead of frightening people, this fish makes everyone want it for a pet because it is so beautiful. It is very often used in salt water home aquariums.

Isn't it too bad the peaceful Manta Ray was born with ugly horns and acts as if it were so mean when snared, for if it were beautiful and "smiling" like the Angelfish, people wouldn't be so afraid of it.

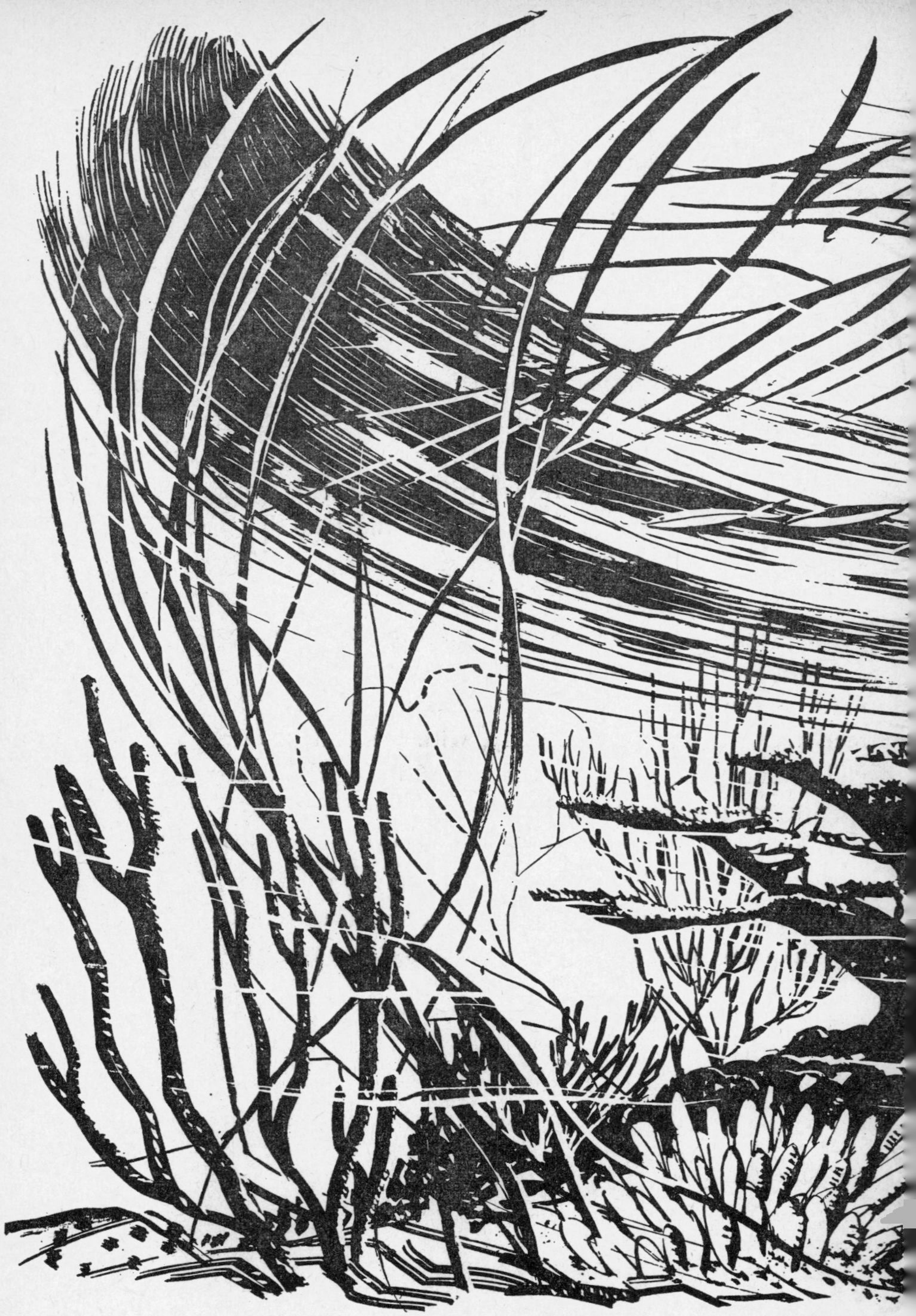

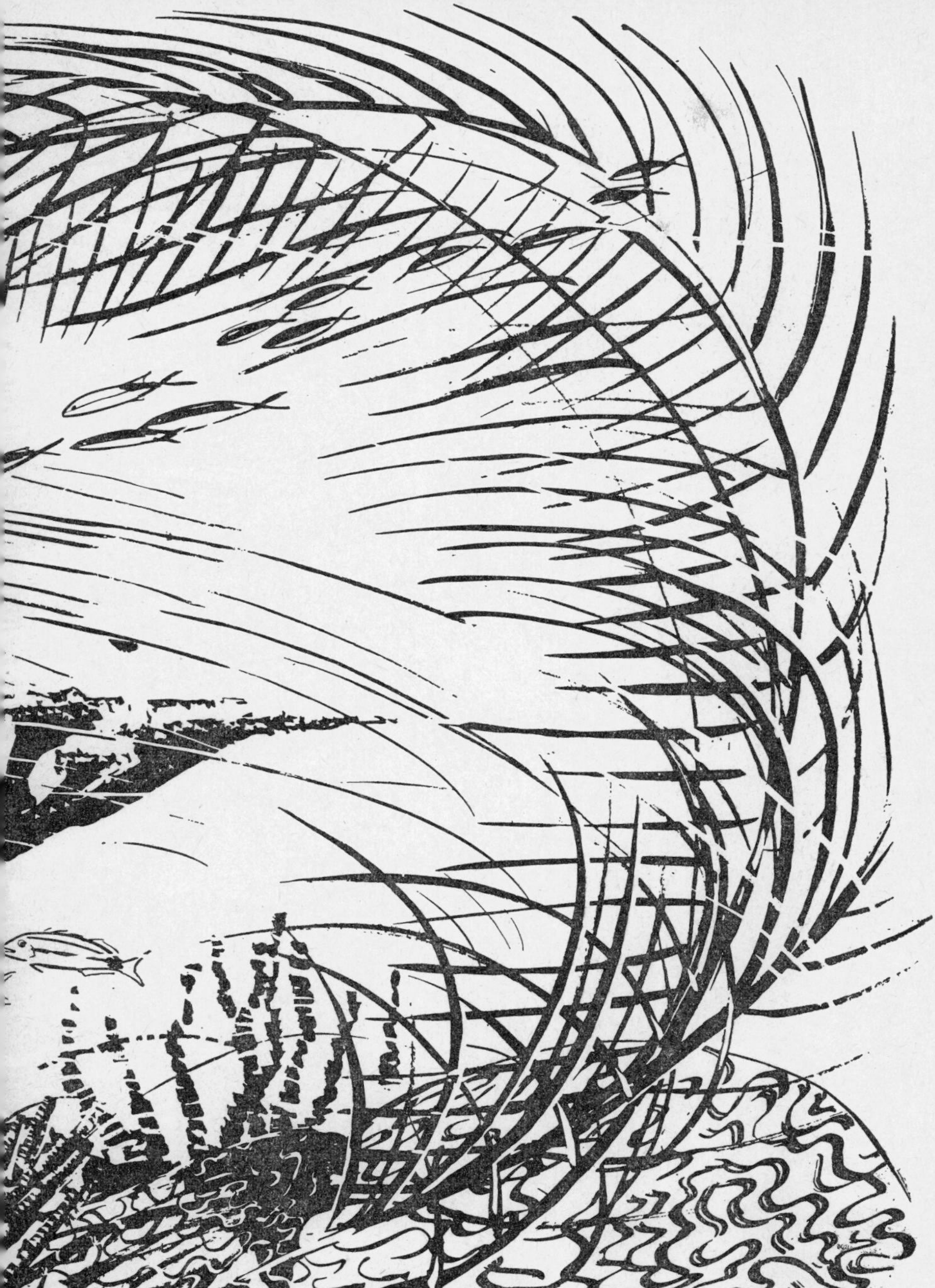

# Humuhumu Nukunuku Apua-a

If you try to say this Hawaiian name for the Queen Trigger Fish very fast, you will get your tongue all twisted just as if you said, "She sells sea shells by the seashore." Translated and broken down *Humuhumu* means a needle or spine, *Nukunuku* means the snout of *Apua-a,* which is a pig. Altogether *Humuhumu Nukunuku Apua-a* means the fish with a needle or spine that has a snout like a pig. But this fish certainly does not look like a pig,·for with its bright bands of blue, yellow, green and black, it is one of the most beautiful and highly colored inhabitants of the ocean.

The Queen Trigger Fish is found in the South Seas, near Hawaii, and in other warm ocean areas of the world. It has one interesting trick from which it gets its name. When in danger, it hides in a hole in a reef. Erecting the strong spine on its back, together with a similar spine on its stomach, it wedges itself in firmly. No matter how hard a large fish might pull, the Trigger Fish cannot be budged. But humans have found one way to get this fish loose which is very clever. You touch the third spine on its back, pushing down on it as if it were a trigger on a gun. This immediately releases the strong, erect first spine which is holding the creature wedged in its hole. Then the Trigger Fish can easily be pulled out of its fortress.

Many a hungry fish in the ocean that has tried to eat the *Humuhumu Nukunuku Apua-a* has probably wished that it had left the creature alone, because if the spine is erect while being swallowed the gobbler gets a nasty cut in its throat, since it is unable to work the secret combination of the third spine "trigger."

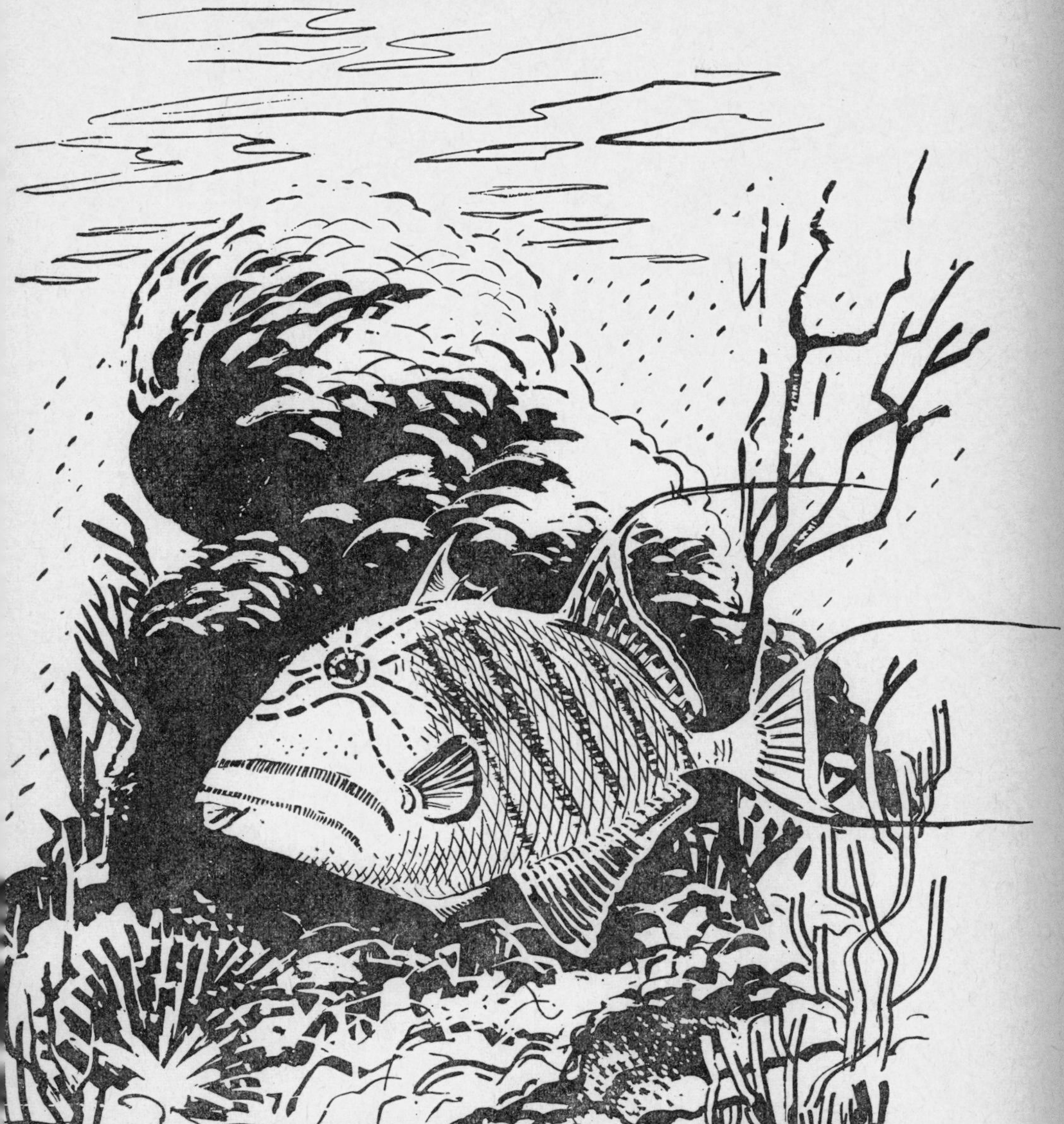

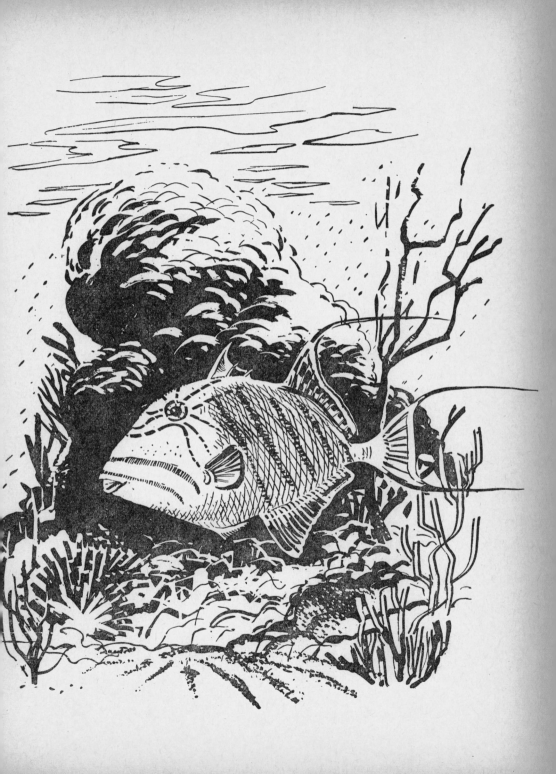

# Sky Fishes

Just because some sea animals have names that make us think of the sky does not mean that they come from there or that they are as beautiful as the stars, moon and sun, for, even dressed up with fancy names, many of these Sky Fishes are very funny looking.

The Sun Fish is like the sun in only one respect — it is round and big. It has a remarkable shape, even for a fish, with a deep circular and somewhat thin body, appearing as though the tail part had been cut off. This makes it look as if it were all head and no tail and for this reason it is also called the Headfish.

Drifting with the currents and basking on the surface of the ocean, a Sun Fish leads a lazy life. It swims so slowly that it could never get out of the way of an enemy, so it is equipped with a thick, leathery skin which serves as protection. It grows to be eight feet long and can weigh as much as a ton — which also might discourage any other fish from attacking it! By taking long dives, the Sun Fish is able to get its favorite food of deep-sea fishes. It is called a stupid fish — probably because it is so sluggish in comparison to the many fast fishes that go zooming all around it.

Starfish have been given this name because they have arms which look like the points of a star. Some have five arms, while others have as many as fifty. Each arm has hundreds of suckers which act as feet as it moves slowly along the ocean bottom. It is no problem at all for a Starfish to grow new arms in case the old ones are torn off.

Some full-grown Starfish are as small as a dime or as big as two feet across the arm spread, and they live in both deep and shallow water, in rocks or on the sandy bottom. They may be smooth or rough, and they come in many colors. A Starfish has no head but its mouth and stomach are located in a strange place — underneath it!

Starfish have an enormous number of eggs, which are so small that it is almost impossible to see them with your naked eye. These are left in the water to drift with the currents. The female Starfish never sees its offspring and probably does not know that a great number of these eggs are eaten by creatures of the sea. Only a few will be left to grow into mature Starfish.

All kinds of small animals are eaten by Starfish, but they especially like oysters. They open the hard oyster shell by pulling, slowly and steadily, with the suckers on their arms. The oyster finally gives up, loosens the muscle holding its shell, and the Starfish thrusts its elastic stomach inside the shell and eats the oyster.

There is one peculiar thing that Starfish do. They will join their arms together and ball up in a great mass, hundreds of them together. No one seems to know exactly why they do this. Perhaps it is to keep warm or maybe they join forces when an enemy threatens. They might have found out that they are stronger together than when they are alone.

Moon Fish are very flat, thin fish with almost round bodies, about the size of a dinner plate. They eat all kinds of smaller fish, live mostly near docks and bridges in warm seas, and belong to the Jack family. They usually come out at night and if the beam of a flashlight shines through the water on their silvery bodies, it gives them the appearance of small moons.

The long fins of the Moon Fish make them look very beautiful, but the profile of the head is odd because it seems as if the forehead drops straight down to the mouth!

The Star Gazer is a stout, clumsy fish with a box-shaped head, which is found in the shallow water of warm oceans. It is unable to swim fast enough to chase the small fish on which it feeds, so it resorts to cunning in order to get its food. It buries itself in the sand of the ocean floor so that only its small eyes and the upper part of its mouth-opening are sticking out. It is perfectly camouflaged to look like a gray stone.

While the Star Gazer lies quietly, it sticks a red tongue-like piece of flesh out of its mouth. It moves this about in the sand, making it crawl, wriggle, contract and expand — imitating to perfection the movements of a small worm. This is its lure or bait and, sooner or later, a small, hungry fish starts to pick up what it believes to be an attractive red worm. Immediately, the concealed jaws of the Star Gazer grab the fish dinner.

## Salt Water Dragons

Before you hear about the vicious Salt Water Crocodile, you should try to learn the difference between an Alligator and a Crocodile, because these two water-dwelling reptiles are closely related, look very much alike and are often mistaken for one another.

An Alligator lives in fresh and brackish water of tropical countries and will mind its own business and even run from you — unless, of course, it is injured, molested or guarding its nest of eggs, which it usually keeps hidden in a cave in the mud. But the Salt Water Crocodile that is found in brackish waters is a vicious, dangerous animal that will go out of its way to attack. It is known as a man-eater and has been responsible for many deaths.

The Crocodile's head is narrow and pointed and it has enormous, sharp teeth in its ugly, powerful jaws. Two of these teeth in the lower jaw stick up bulldog fashion, adding to its mean-looking appearance. Its blackish-colored, horny body can grow as long as thirty-three feet, which makes it the largest of living reptiles. The powerful tail, shaped flat like that of a fish, is used for swimming and helps to propel the animal faster than you can paddle a canoe. A Crocodile looks like the wicked dragons you have seen in fairy tale picture books.

The Alligator's head is not as narrow and pointed as the Crocodile's. It has an olive or gray, horny body and tail and it has a greater number of teeth set in its powerful jaws than the Crocodile. You can probably see that to an inexperienced person both the Alligator and the Crocodile may look somewhat alike.

Even though you think you know the difference between these reptiles, it would *not* be a good idea to come close to an Alligator and say *Boo!* and try to scare it away. It might be a female Alligator with young ones, and attack you. Or you *could* be near a vicious Crocodile, after all, so it is best to stay away from both of them.

Luckily, the Salt Water Crocodile is not found all over the world, but only in the regions extending from Bengal, India, to South China, and in North Australia and the Fiji Islands. It very often swims far into the ocean, out of sight of land, or it may be found in the mud flats and mangrove swamps of brackish estuaries and salt marshes.

Natives who live in the countries where the Salt Water Crocodile is found are always on the lookout when they go swimming or are out in a boat. Very often, what appears to be a log turns out to be a Crocodile!

The male Crocodile bellows loudly during mating season, and the female lays her white, oval, thick-shelled eggs on shore. The heat helps to incubate them. When a baby Crocodile is ready to come out of the egg, it gives a hiccough-like cry and breaks through the shell with its egg tooth — a slight bump on the tip of the snout. This egg tooth drops off after the babies hatch, for they no longer have any use for it. The newborn Crocodiles are able to take care of themselves right away and are as mean as their parents. Their tough hides give good protection, for if a foolish fish should attempt to bite a Crocodile, it would surely break its teeth — that is, if the fish could get close enough even to try.

Salt Water Crocodiles are often hunted for their hides, which are made into tough leather and used for shoes, suitcases and many other useful things.

Once a Crocodile's jaws have been clamped shut by their powerful muscles, there is absolutely nothing, short of death, which will open them again — unless the Crocodile itself wants to. But you can keep the Crocodile from *opening* its mouth by a very simple trick. You pinch down on the top and bottom jaw with your fingers, holding on to the tip of the nose with one hand. You see, a Crocodile has terrific power to *close* its jaws but is very weak when it comes to *opening* them. You must remember this, for if you ever go Crocodile hunting, it might come in handy!

## *Fish That Fly*

All of us would like to have wings and be able to fly. To be a combination of flying bird and swimming fish seems almost too good to be true. Well, there is one inhabitant of the deep ocean that is just such a combination. It is a Flying Fish, which grows to a length of ten inches, is a beautiful silver and blue color and looks like any ordinary fish, but with one difference — it has fins shaped like wings. Besides this, it has an air bladder which takes up more than half of its body and acts like a balloon, making the fish very light, so that it can come flying out of the water or go swimming back into it, as it wishes.

Flying Fish are found in all the warm seas and they are delicious to eat. Fishermen often catch them in large nets, rarely on a hook and line. Sometimes, if you place a strong light close to the water at night, you may attract a school of Flying Fish. The light seems to excite the fish and they fly in all directions, as if they were having the time of their lives. In this way, they will often jump right into a fisherman's arms.

While these agile fish are still babies, they learn to fly, just as their parents do. These young ones look like brown grasshoppers as they skim gracefully over the ocean, playing submarine and airplane.

Being a combination of bird and fish is a pretty good trick in itself, but the Flying Fish has more important needs for this ability. Sometimes when a large, hungry fish is chasing it, there just isn't anywhere to hide down below, so the Flying Fish swims very fast to the surface and hurls itself from the water. Once in the air, it stretches its wings out and glides, often as far as two hundred feet, and in this way can escape the enemy that lurks below.

But the Flying Fish is not always able to make a getaway, for often there are large sea birds waiting in the air above, and these are quick to make a meal of it.

It makes you wonder whether, if the Flying Fish had its choice, it would be a full-time bird or a full-time fish, or is it happiest just as it is?

# Poison Fish

Did you know that there is a certain fish in the ocean which is deadlier than a rattlesnake or a cobra? It is a member of the Scorpion Fish family and is found in the South Seas and Australia. Here it lives in shallow, rocky places, and because it looks so much like its surroundings, it is called a Stonefish.

Besides being very dangerous, it is also one of the ugliest looking creatures on earth. It has warty, wrinkled skin all over its body, the lower jaw sticks out in a mean stubborn way, and its two small eyes are set close together and can hardly be seen in the many folds of skin. Hidden on its back, in the loose skin, are thirteen wicked, bluish colored spines, each one containing two sacs of deadly poison. If something presses against these needle-sharp spines, they immediately inject their poison, causing violent pain and sometimes death.

A poisonous snake on land can usually be seen and avoided but the dull-colored Stonefish is so well camouflaged, looking like a piece of dead coral or crumbling rock, that it is difficult to see. It lies motionless in the sand, alongside of some real coral, and in those parts of the world where this venomous creature is found, waders must be careful where they step. Fortunately, this fish does not go out of its way looking for trouble, but uses its poison only for protection.

The most interesting thing about the Stonefish is that if its poison is not fatal, it does some very peculiar things to people. While you are recovering from the painful stabs of the dorsal spines, everything hot that you eat will taste cold and everything cold that you eat will taste hot. If you touch ice, your hand will feel as if it were on fire. If you burn your hand, you will think it is freezing. Can't you just see yourself blowing on your ice cream because you think it is too hot, or refusing to eat hot soup, telling your mother it is ice cold?

# Prehistoric Monsters

Millions of years ago, the ocean was filled with many weird creatures. Some had huge bodies with funny long necks, and others looked like ferocious serpents with sharp teeth. Of all these fantastic animals only a few have survived through the ages and can still be found in the ocean. One is the Green Sea Turtle which, though rarely longer than four feet, often weighs a thousand pounds. It is covered with heart-shaped armor of heavy shell, both on top and underneath. This protects its body so that it is difficult for any other animal to harm it.

Even in these modern times, the Green Sea Turtle still lives in the same way as its ancestors did so many years ago. It eats fish, grass and jellyfish, swims in the deep places of the ocean, where it can stay under water for pretty nearly an hour, and sometimes suns itself on the surface.

But the most remarkable thing about these prehistoric animals is the way they have laid their eggs since the beginning of time. Each year, the females swim the vast ocean until a suitable spot is found on the shore of some warm country. Here, usually at night, they crawl up on the beach to lay their eggs. They make slow progress from the ocean to the dry sand, laboring and struggling under the weight of their heavy shells.

When you see a Green Sea Turtle ponderously come out of the ocean, it is such a huge, strange-looking monster that you want to run out of its way. But these Turtles are harmless and if you stand quietly and watch, with a flashlight to help, you will see one of the wonders of Nature take place right before your eyes.

As soon as the Turtle has reached a desirable location on the dry sand, above the high tide line, it uses its flippers to scoop out a very deep hole, into which it lays its eggs. These look like white ping-pong balls and very often the mother Turtle lays two hundred of them in a night. Then, very carefully, again using its flippers, the Turtle covers the eggs with sand and slowly crawls back to the sea. You can always tell where a

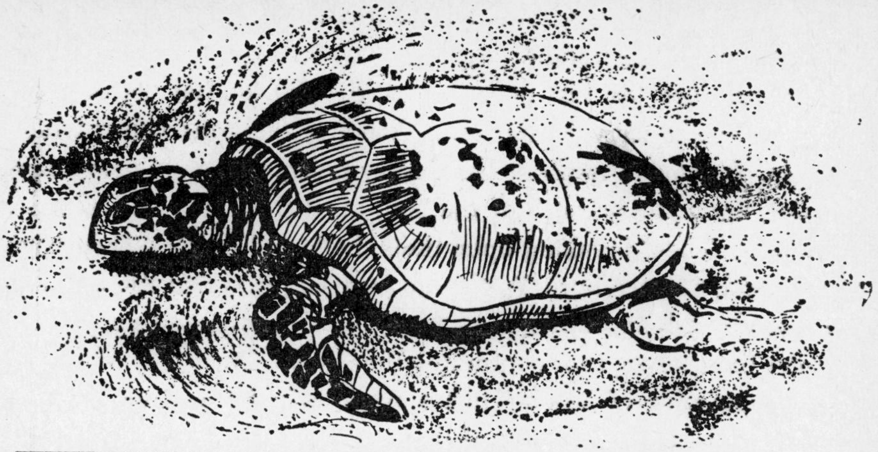
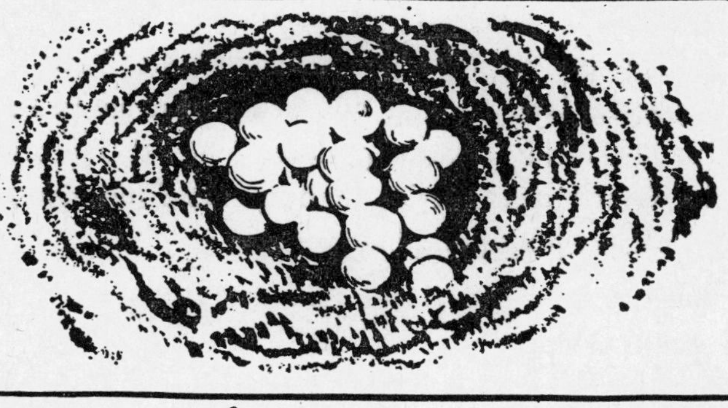
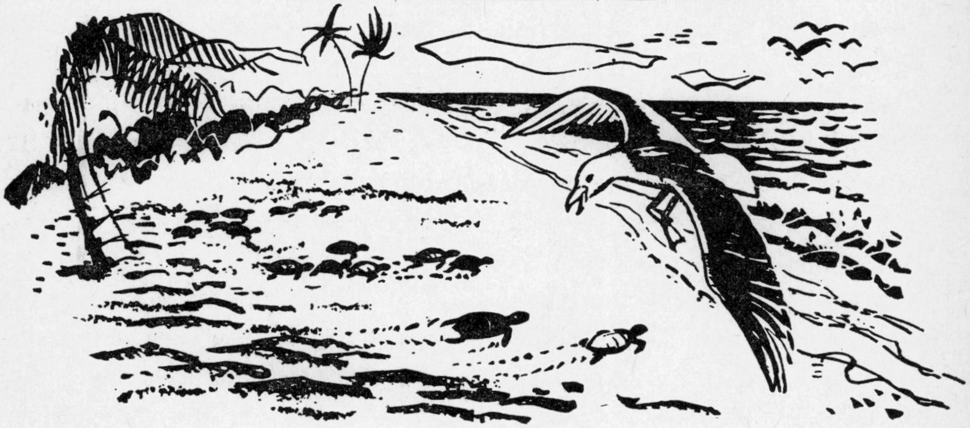

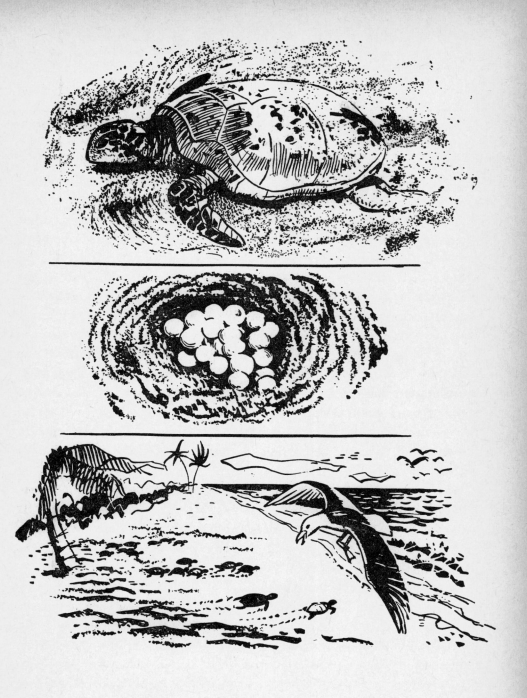

Turtle has laid its eggs, for it leaves tracks in the sand which look like those of a miniature tractor.

The sun does the rest of the work for the mother Turtle. It shines down on the nursery in the sand, keeping the eggs warm while they develop. It takes anywhere from forty-seven to seventy-two days, depending upon the warmth of the sun, until the baby Turtles are ready to be born. Then, breaking open their shells and digging themselves out of the sand, the newborn Turtles go hurrying down to the ocean. Many are eaten by fish and birds, but others live to grow into large Turtles and lay eggs themselves, thus continuing the cycle.

For thousands of years Turtles were safe from most of the other animals in the ocean because of their tough shells. Then man discovered that Turtles and their eggs were good to eat and it was easy to get them when they came up on the sand at spawning time. That is why some countries have passed laws so that no one is allowed to take the eggs and kill the Turtles during certain periods. With this protection, there will perhaps be Green Sea Turtles many years from now, still laying their eggs that look like ping-pong balls.

# The Fish That Changes Its Face

Life must be very embarrassing to a Halibut, for when it is about six months old, its face changes so that even its own mother would not recognize it. When it is first hatched out of an egg, it looks like any other ordinary fish, with its eyes where they should be, one on each side of its face. Then a remarkable transformation takes place and the Halibut's left eye, together with the snout, gradually move over to the right side of its head, until it looks like an entirely different fish from the one it used to be.

This is the way the young Halibut is prepared for its life on the bottom of the sea, where it will stay most of the time. With its sandy colored back, and eyes always looking upward, other fishes have difficulty seeing it. But the camouflaged Halibut can easily see the other fishes.

A female Halibut lays several million eggs at a time. This arrangement is a good one because so many of the eggs, as well as the young fish, are eaten before they have a chance to reach maturity, and with such large numbers, there will always be some left.

During the early part of their lives, before their faces change, Halibuts drift with the currents in great schools, milling around and eating small sea life. But as they grow older and leave the schools, each one settles down to its own life, which is mostly a question of how to catch enough food every day and how to keep from being caught as food itself.

Some Halibut live to an old age, often growing as big as three hundred pounds, and considering the number of fishermen who try to catch them, these are pretty lucky fish.

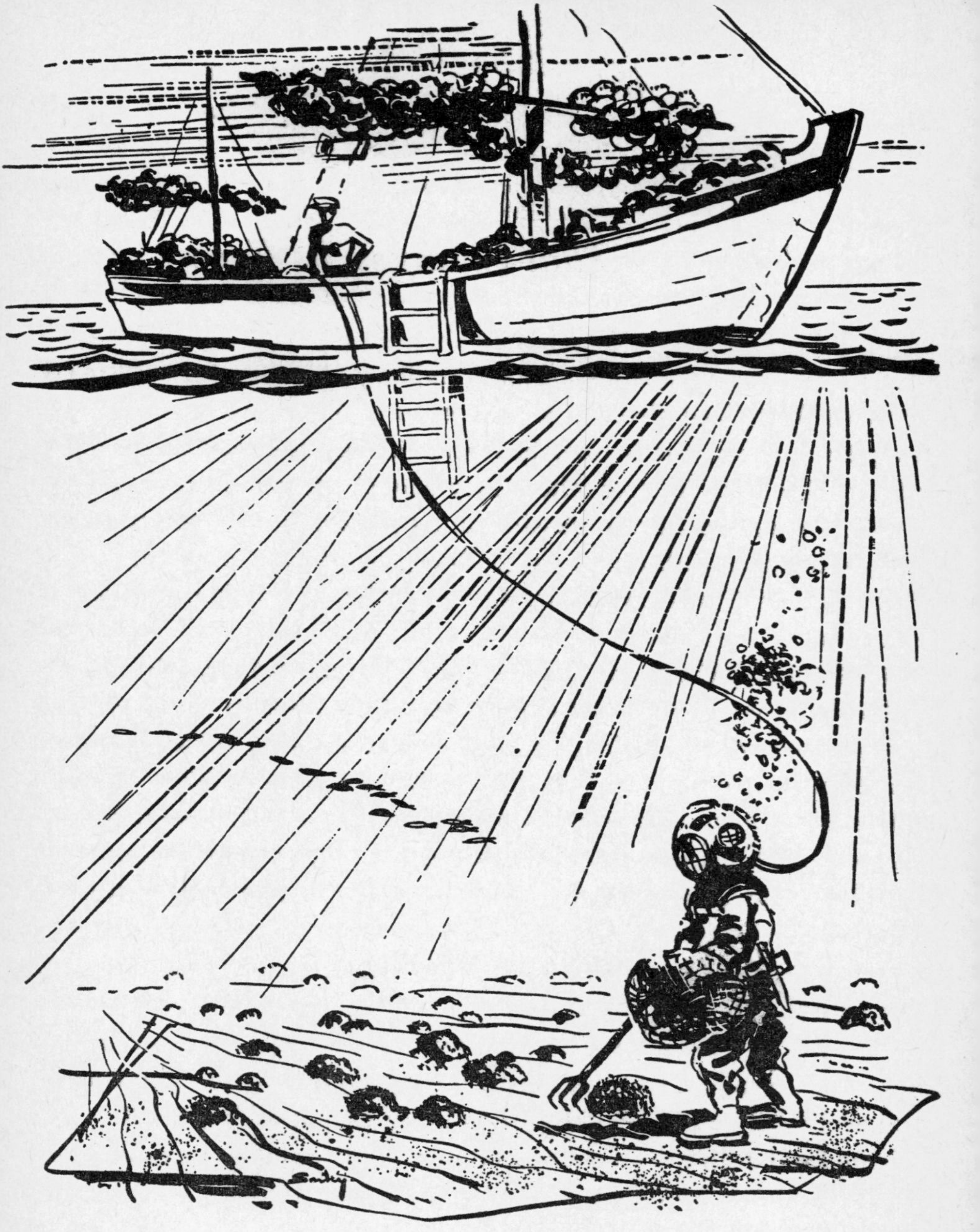

# Skeletons That Wash Cars

There is a living animal in the ocean called a Sponge whose body is mostly holes and which looks very much like a honeycomb. Through some of these holes the Sponge breathes, and through others it eats. Although the Sponge has no mouth, teeth or stomach, it seems to get along very well by straining minute sea-life out of the water through these holes. When you buy a Sponge in a store, you are really planning to use only its skeleton for washing purposes. This is soft and pliable and absorbs a great amount of water.

Some kinds of Sponges are found in almost every ocean, living in shallow or deep places, either where it is warm or cold. They are peace-loving and none of the animals in the ocean try to eat them, because their taste and smell is so very unpleasant.

As soon as a Sponge is born, it attaches itself to a rock and here it stays all its life. But often, if it cannot find a rock, it grabs on to the shell of a convenient Hermit Crab or Sea Snail. As the Sponge grows larger, it does not mean to do so, but it often kills these animals with its weight.

In Greece and Florida, where most Sponge beds are found, it takes a great deal of work — and it is sometimes dangerous — to find Sponges on the ocean floor. The Sponge fishermen steer their brightly painted boat toward the hunting grounds, which are often great distances from their home port. The boat is anchored and the divers climb overboard, descending deep into the water. They wear diver's suits and helmets, and air is pumped to them from the ship above.

Down in the ocean, the sponge diver walks slowly along the bottom, carrying a wire basket which is attached to the boat above by a long rope. He pulls the Sponges off the bottom and fills his basket, then gives a signal to the men on the boat to hoist it up.

Sometimes a diver faces great danger when an eel, hiding in the rocks, darts out at him or a shark attacks him. This is why Sponge divers are always armed with a sharp knife.

At last the boat has a full load of Sponges. They are everywhere —
above and below the decks. Then comes the job of preparing them for
the Sponge market.

You would hardly recognize the clean Sponges you use at home in the
objects that first come up from the ocean. They are black and oozing
with live little worms and small marine animals. Skilled hands work and
knead the Sponge until all of these come scurrying out. Then, after
scraping and rinsing many times, the flesh of the Sponge comes away
from the skeleton. Finally, the latter is trimmed evenly, bleached and
dried, by exposing it to the sun. After all this preparation, the only thing
that remains of the Sponge is its skeleton, and this is what you finally
buy in your neighborhood store, using it to wash yourself or your car or
for many other useful purposes.

# Ocean Clowns

The next time you are at the circus, take a good look at the clowns who have permanent smiles painted on their faces. Then you will know why the Porpoise is called the Clown of the Sea, for its face, too, looks as if it were fixed in a stationary smile. Besides, a Porpoise appears to be performing and doing tricks, just as if it were in the circus. It races across the surface of the water, jumps, dives and rolls on its back over and over again, and never seems to tire of having fun.

While playing in this way, the Porpoise is also taking in gulps of fresh air, for this sea creature has lungs just as we have. It cannot stay under water for any length of time, as most other ocean animals can, for it is a mammal — you know, an animal that nourishes its young — and it must hold its breath while down there, coming up for air every minute or so.

Porpoises usually travel together in large, friendly groups and they like nothing better than to follow a ship, playing tag with it. They allow the vessel to get ahead and then, with a great burst of speed, they race forward. It almost looks as if they were showing off to the people aboard and proving that they can travel as fast as thirty miles an hour.

When a baby Porpoise is born, it is three feet in length and, being a mammal, it nurses. It does not take long for the baby to grow as big as its fourteen-foot father. If anything happens to the newborn's mother, the other females will take good care of it, protecting it from danger.

Baby Porpoises, just like their parents, are very curious and show their love of fun. One five-week-old youngster delighted in poking its nose into a fish's cave and teasing it into backing away. Then, rushing around to the back door, the baby would start nipping at the poor fish's tail, trying to force it out the front. This went on hour after hour.

Perhaps some day, if you have a salt water swimming pool, you might keep a Porpoise as a pet; for as well as being playful, it is easy to train. It will jump high out of the water after food and can be taught to come swimming up at your signal, to be petted and to have its head rubbed.

Who knows, you might even put a leash around its neck and be able to lead it around the pool.

Even though Porpoises are usually very good-natured, they do not allow other animals of the sea to take advantage of them. Their large mouths have rows of sharp teeth and they do not hesitate to use them. When they get into a school of small fish, they cause a panic by eating enormous numbers of them.

Many years ago, the Porpoise was used for food, but now it is only in France that people still eat them. This has worked out fine for the Porpoises because, not being bothered, they have been able to multiply so that the ocean is full of them.

It is believed that Porpoises will save a drowning man from sharks by surrounding him in defensive formation and pushing him to shore. This has never been proven, even though the agile creatures have been seen more than once pushing ashore an unconscious human being. But this could be some kind of game with them and they might not even know that they are doing life-guard duty.

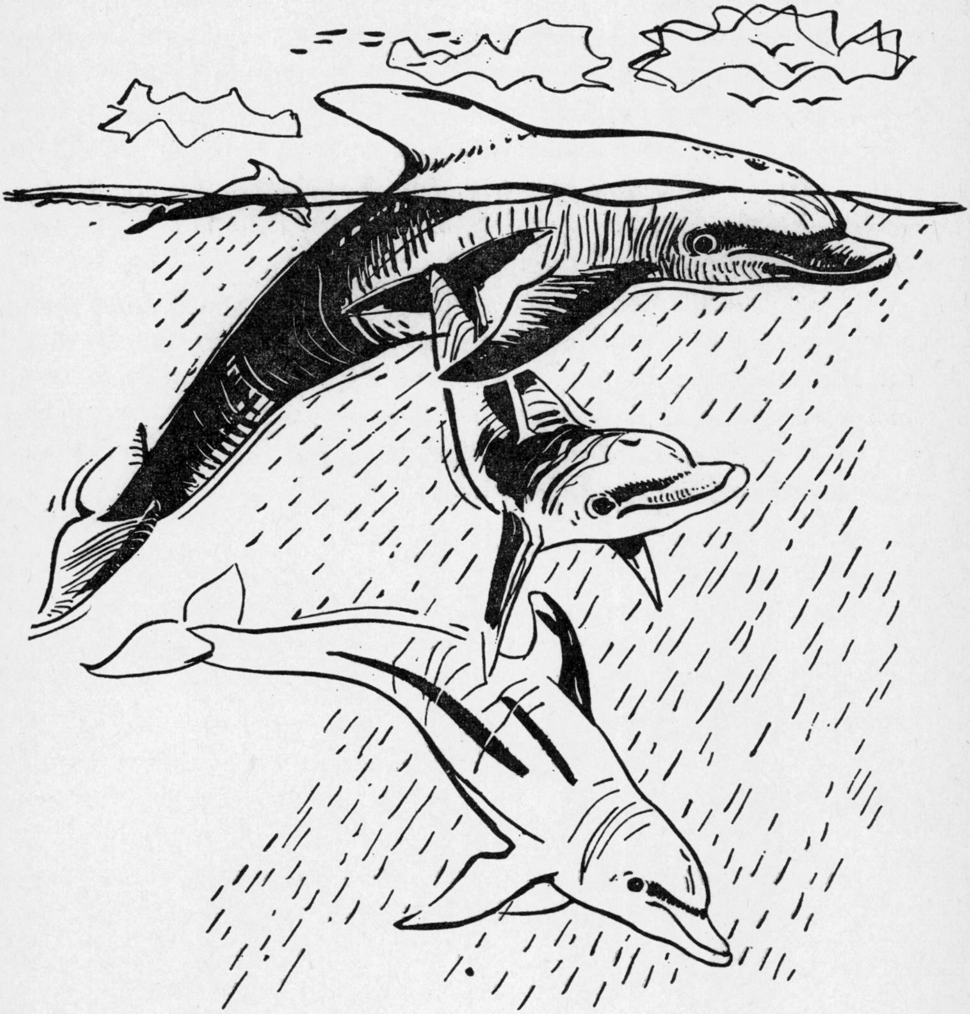

## Swellfishes

If you want to play catch on the beach and don't have a ball, you might find a Porcupine Fish washed ashore which could be used. This fish inflates itself with so much air or water that it swells up as round and almost as big as a volleyball. Its skin becomes so tight that it looks as if it would burst. Of course, you would first have to shave off the spines sticking out all over in this makeshift ball — and Porcupine Fish are not so easy to find, either. So perhaps you had better wait until you can use a real ball, after all.

There are many varieties of Porcupine Fishes in most waters of the world. They are not able to swim very well and cannot move quickly enough to get out of the way of their enemies, so they puff up like balloons for protection. What large ocean fish would be foolish enough to gobble down a spiny balloon? If it tried, the Porcupine Fish would certainly stick in its throat. For this reason, these Swellfish float lazily on top of the water, drifting with the currents, upside down, knowing full well they are safe.

Baby Porcupine Fish have a cute trick that is used as protection during times of danger. They all move close together and blow themselves up, which makes them look like one large, prickly fish, too big for any sea creature to swallow.

If you ever catch a Porcupine Fish while fishing, and it is not already puffed up, you can tickle its stomach and back with a stick and soon it will be as big as a balloon. Then throw it back into the water and it will float just like a cork.

In the islands of the South Seas, the natives dry the spiny skins of the Porcupine Fish for use as war helmets. And in Japan they make lanterns out of them by putting candles inside. The light shines through the stretched skin, making an interesting homemade lantern.

One close relative of the Porcupine Fish is a puffer fish, which lives in Japanese waters and is very poisonous to eat. You will hardly believe it, but the natives use them to make a delicious soup, in spite of the fact that many get very ill from eating it!

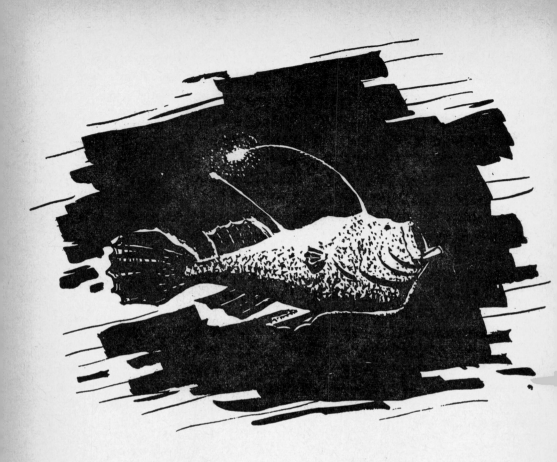

## Swimming Light Bulbs

The deeper down in the ocean you go, the darker it becomes. If it should be your good luck to descend in a diving bell — a hollow steel ball with windows which is lowered from the side of a ship by cables — you will find it is as dark as night, even before you are a mile down beneath the surface. It is so very black that even fishes have trouble seeing. This problem has been solved in a unique way.

Many of the creatures that live in these inky depths are luminescent — meaning they light up very much like electric bulbs. A certain substance that these fishes manufacture enables them to turn their electricity on and off just as easily as you would operate a wall switch in your home. They use their remarkable lights to attract food or a mate, to identify themselves to their own kind, or as a defense with which to frighten or confuse their enemies.

If you have ever seen an automobile being driven at night without headlights (which you probably haven't, because practically no one is foolish enough to do this), then you must know how these fishes react in the dark, deep ocean. They would never be able to see one another, even a few inches away, without their lights, and they might have one head-on collision after another.

One peculiar six-foot-long fish has been named by explorer, Dr. William Beebe, the Untouchable Bathysphere Fish. It has its lighting organs dangling from beneath its body — one from the lower jaw, the other below its tail. This fish also has lights along its body which look very much like the glowing portholes of a ship at night.

Still another odd one is the Deep Sea Angler Fish. The females have a fishing rod attached to their heads and the tips of these rods glow like light bulbs. It is believed that this is the way they attract food — a fish that goes fishing!

Another creature in this black underwater world waits until a tasty fish passes by, then quickly flashes its light directly at the bewildered fish's face. If you want to know how this feels, just have someone point a flashlight directly into your eyes on a dark night. Of course, the fish that was just passing by is gulped down for a meal while still surprised and blinded by the strong light.

Perhaps the queerest looking of all the deep water dwellers is a certain fish that has a stalk sticking out below its eye, on the end of which is a lighting organ, glowing like a torch. When it wants to put out the light, it curls up this stalk, tucking it neatly into a small pouch built in the skin.

Very little is really known about all these strange fishes because no one has been able to stay down long enough to study them at the depths where they are found. But the little that *is* known about them reminds us of a strange, fantastic almost unknown world.

## *Carpenter Tools That Don't Work*

The names Sawfish and Hammerhead Shark, which belong to two fishes whose heads are different from any others in the ocean, would make you think that they are useful to a carpenter in his work. But this is not so, for they are useful to man in a way entirely different from tools.

The Sawfish may grow to twenty feet, and all of this great length of skin is made into a tough leather. Its liver yields a valuable oil, and in some countries the fins are made into soup. And the double-edged saw on the end of its nose, which often grows to be six feet long, is used as a curio.

This remarkable saw, after which the Sawfish is named, is used to grub about in the sand and mud for crabs and other creatures lying buried. And when it runs upon a school of fish, the Sawfish uses this terrific weapon on its nose to strike rapidly from side to side, killing or stunning its food before it eats. Fishermen have had frightening experiences with this huge monster that often grows to weigh as much as two and a half tons. With such great weight, the creature can drive its saw into a boat's hull, break it off there and then swim away, leaving it stuck in the wood. Perhaps it is showing off, to prove that the saw on its nose is dangerous, for, actually the Sawfish is not a mean fish.

The Hammerhead Shark *is* a vicious fish and it is considered a man-eater in most parts of the world. It really fits the part, too, for its head spreads out on each side, making it look as dangerous as a double-bladed ax or hammer. The eyes are on the very ends of these ax blades, sometimes three feet apart. This hammer-head acts as a forward rudder, en-

abling the fish to maneuver more skillfully than other sharks.

Growing so large that it may weigh fifteen hundred pounds and measure fifteen feet long, the Hammerhead Shark eats great quantities of other fishes, as well as squids. This huge animal is valuable to man, though, for its skin is made into leather, which in turn is fashioned into shoes and many other things.

A Hammerhead Shark usually has twenty-five to thirty babies at a time. The female keeps the eggs inside her body until they are mature. As soon as the baby Hammerheads are born they are able to swim. Their heads look like a handful of floating toy hammers bobbling along beside their big mother.

If you should be out deep-sea fishing with your father one day, and a Hammerhead Shark or Sawfish grabs the bait, you will have the most exciting time of your life, for these huge fishes put up a terrific fight. They can tow a boat for miles as they struggle to get rid of the hook. They only give up when they are completely exhausted.

## The Backward Swimming Animal

How would you like to go backward always in order to move really fast? Or to be so silly that you would deliberately enter a wire trap through a hole and never find the way out again? These are some of the things a Crayfish does that are not so bright, but in other ways it is quite smart. For instance, the way it sticks out its two long, sensitive feelers from its hiding place in the rocks in order to discover whether there is any danger lurking out there before it emerges. And how it swims and fights by flapping its tail quickly back and forth. Crayfish have to be very careful, for they are so good to eat that both men and sea animals are forever trying to catch them.

Crayfish, also known as Spiny Lobsters, are found in all warm waters of the world, where they live in coral reefs and rocks. They are reddish-brown and grow to a length of sixteen inches. They do not have the enormous claws of the Maine lobster, but the female does have small claws on her hindmost legs, and all Crayfish are covered with a thorn-like protective shell.

When Crayfish eggs hatch, the babies look very funny. They are broad and flat, thin as paper and transparent as glass. They have spidery legs and large black eyes on long stalks. Although they change appearances when they become adult, they always remain queer-looking.

Crayfish can crawl on the ocean bottom with their long, spindly legs, but in order to move fast, they must clap the tail downward toward the body. This pushes the water away and propels them backward. It is very much like when you push the water away from you with your hands in order to swim. The only trouble with this kind of fast traveling is that it makes the Crayfish go backward instead of forward.

Even this backward swimming does not help Crayfish out of the wire cages that are set for them along the coral reefs. During the day they crawl into these traps and bunch up, and then, when night comes and they are ready to feed, they cannot find the way out. This is the way commercial crayfishermen are able to capture them so that everyone can enjoy eating one of the most delicious foods in the ocean.

## Horses of the Deep

If any fishes in the ocean should feel the urge to play cowboys and
Indians, they would have their own little Sea Horses. However, these
steeds of the sea wouldn't trot or gallop on command, and probably they
wouldn't even want to play because the little Sea Horses are very shy
fish that much prefer hiding in the weeds, minding their own business.
But when you look at one, with its horse-like head held high, you might
well think that a baby thoroughbred was lost at sea.

A completely horse-like animal beneath the water would be very un-usual and attract too much attention from marauding neighbors so the rest of the Sea Horse's body is more like a fish. It also resembles some sea plants. Instead of scales, it has a coat of flexible armor, and it seldom grows to be longer than ten inches. If you look closely, you can spot it in an upright position, with the very tip of its tail hanging on to a weed as it sways to and fro with the current.

These little horses of the deep are found in all oceans of the world and they like nothing better than a meal of very tiny minnows or shrimp. The most interesting thing about them is the way they bring their young into the world.

The mother Sea Horse lays her eggs, as do most fish, but not just any-where. She deposits several hundred of them in a special sac-like pouch that her husband has for this purpose. After fertilizing the eggs, he takes care of them for a while in this pouch. Once they hatch, though, father and mother Sea Horse are no longer responsible for what happens to their babies. Like most other fishes in the ocean, they must learn at an early age to shift for themselves.

Perhaps it is a good thing that the Sea Horse is a silent fish, for if it neighed like a real horse, it would get itself into all kinds of trouble. Silence is a valuable habit at the bottom of the sea. One small sound might give away a hiding place and cause quick death in the jaws of a larger fish. But by remaining quiet, and by being well camouflaged so as to look like a water plant, the Sea Horse usually escapes the quick eyes of hungry fishes.

# Big Serpents

Some time ago a ship was sailing along off the coast of Ireland when suddenly its crew saw something that filled them with fear. It was a gigantic creature that rose out of the ocean depths right in front of their ship, and for a few moments they thought it would ram into the vessel and capsize it. This huge animal had a small, snake-like head, and on each side of its body there were a pair of paddles that looked like the flippers of a seal, only much larger. But the most terrifying part about this monster was its size! All who saw it claimed it was sixty feet in length, twenty feet of which was a long slender neck. If you placed three automobiles end to end, it would show you how long the sailors said the monster was, and you might get some idea of why these men felt so frightened.

The strange creature did not damage the ship and it soon disappeared beneath the water, just as mysteriously as it had appeared. After the crewmen came to their senses and realized they were still alive and safe, they proceeded to give thanks, and then sent a message by wireless which read: "Sea Serpent sighted again."

Almost this same thing has occurred for more than one hundred and fifty years, in most waters of the world. At least once each year men near or on the ocean have seen an awesome creature which they call a Sea Serpent, and all who have seen these monsters have given very nearly the same description of them. They seem to be from twenty to one hundred and seventy-five feet in length and their bodies are either smooth or scaly. They have long necks and heads like snakes, and their tails taper to a point. They are said to have either one or two pairs of flippers.

Some scientists doubt that Sea Serpents exist and claim that there might be explanations for them, such as long, thick strands of seaweed torn loose from the deep ocean bottom and floating on the surface, or a large Octopus swimming through the water with its long arms trailing behind it. These might very well look like some strange animal in the water. That is why, until a Sea Serpent is actually brought to shore for people to see and scientists to examine, there is no positive proof that these monsters do exist. Just the same, many times when ships and their crews have disappeared in a dead calm at sea, with no known storm to sink them, their disappearances have been blamed on Sea Serpents.

Some people believe that on the vast stretches of öcean most anything can happen, and in the watery depths any kind of weird creature could be hidden. After all, only about twenty years ago a fish was caught which was supposed to have been extinct for fifty-five million years. This proves we do make mistakes. Who knows, even you might come across a Sea Serpent some day, so whenever you go near the ocean, be sure to take your camera along — just in case.

# *Tailpiece*

Creatures in the sea are not only like animals in the zoo, they are very much like humans, too. They live in special regions of the oceans for very definite reasons, just as we live in special localities on land. For instance, you will find a great assortment of ocean animals where the water is warm and where food is plentiful, just as you will find a great number of people in fertile valleys and plains where the climate is moderate and good soil and rains make food easy to grow.

There are many kinds of sea animals living and feeding in the warm, shallow places near shore, too, for a very good reason. Here plentiful supplies of food may always be found by them, in the shallows, or by digging in the sand. At the same time, these near-shore creatures make their homes in the safety of rocks and coral. Aren't they just like human town-dwellers who live in flats and apartments in large cities and who have all their food, clothing and entertainment right near them, so that they don't have to go long distances to find any of these?

Yes, there *is* a great deal in common between sea creatures and humans. We are all forever hungry, always ready to defend ourselves if someone picks on us, and full of curiosity about anything new and strange.

### Boris Arnov, Jr.

was born in Los Angeles, California, but has spent a great part of his life in Hawaii and Florida. As present he lives in Berkeley, California. He attended Rollins College, in Winter Park, Yale University, Chicago School of Medicine. He also did assistant teaching and research in ichthyology at the Marine Laboratory, University of Miami, Miami, Florida. He owned and operated a charter boat for two years and wrote a weekly fishing column, as well as scientific and popular articles on fish. He is extremely fond of books, boats, and fishing.

### Helen Mather-Smith Mindlin

was born in Kansas City, Missouri, but spent most of her life in California, Hawaii and Florida, with some time in New York, Chicago and St. Louis. At present she lives in Florida. She attended school in both Illinois and California. The author has written scenarios in Hollywood and feature articles for King Features Syndicate and for the *Los Angeles Times Magazine Section*. Older members of the Weekly Reader Book Club remember her thrilling adventure story, *Dangerous Island*, a club selection in 1956. Her interests include not only writing but also yachting, fishing, dogs, wild animals and playing the accordion.